THE GOLDEN BOOK OF
MOROCCO

Raimage
Raissouni Image

BONECHI

CONTENTS

Distributeur pour le Maroc: RAIMAGE Sarl., Angle Rues de Russie et Emsallah, Tél.: 93 42 02, Tanger, Maroc

© Copyright by CASA EDITRICE BONECHI, Via Cairoli, 18/b Florence - Italy
E-mail: bonechi@bonechi.it   Internet: www.bonechi.it

ISBN 88-7009-840-0

• • •

◄ *Outstanding examples of Moroccan crafts.*

Moroccan horsemen participating in the traditional «Fantasia».

INTRODUCTION

A country like Morocco defies description, is more than mere words can tell. One can of course draw up a list of essential facts. But no matter how exhaustive, can such data be anything more than an oversimplified and artificial document?

We can however give it a try.

Morocco, set at the northwestern extremity of the African continent, is bordered by the Mediterranean, the Atlantic Ocean, Algeria and Mauritania. Europe lies practically a stone's throw away, just across the Strait of Gibraltar. At present the population of Morocco numbers somewhat more than 23 million. The climate is temperate to warm. The government is a constitutional democratic and social monarchy which guarantees the plurality of the political parties. Islam is the state religion but freedom of worship is guaranteed. The official language is Arabic.

However a list of this sort, which could be continued and completed ad infinitum, cannot explain how the specific character of this country was formed and what it is. It is not enough to illustrate the results of the slow construction and patient work of time and man. It cannot evoke the beauty of a sunset in Marrakesh or the perfume of the roses which fills the air of Kelaa Megouna in the month of February. No description in words can give us the taste of the mint tea, the bustle of the souks, the generosity manifested on the occasion of the moussem; the feeling of devotion stirred up by a visit to the mausoleum of Mohammed V in Raba or the Zaouia Nassiriya in Tamegroute, the fervor which marked the resistance to foreign occupation in the «Battle of the Three Kings» or during the struggle for independence under the aegis of the man who was still called Sultan Ben Yusuf, the solidarity demonstrated during the construction of the way to unity, the reconstruction of Agadir, after the floods of the Oued Ziz, during the glorious "Green March" or, more recently, the contribution to the construction of the mosque of Hassan II in Casablanca.

This is what Morocco is. A united people, resolute and like-minded. A people ready to accept the challenges presented by their geographic position and their history. In this respect the ruins of Lixus, the town of Moulay Idriss Zerhoun or that of Rissani are much more meaningful than any other modern city. The village of Agdz, firm and staunch in the face of the assault of modernity, reflects eternal Morocco so much better than the seaside resorts on the Mediterranean coast: can a copy compete with the original or be its equal in greatness and wealth? This does not mean that the new, the modern are lacking in beauty, intensity or symbolism, but the soul of the country or a people is not always there where one expects to find it. Casablanca, with its skyscrapers, its broad thoroughfares, represents Morocco of the 20th century, Morocco on the road to progress, Morocco making show of its open-mindedness, its creativity and the commitment of its people. But not even the most sophisticated of computers could ever render an account of the generosity of the Moroccan people, of their legendary hospitality, the wealth of crafts, the variety of culinary arts, their devotion to the sacred values of Islam, the monarchy and the territorial unity. It is a collection of unquantifiable values which elude the predominant logic of modern life. Who would dare to affirm that traditional

3

Morocco is incapable of resisting the depersonalization of modern times? The inhabitants have long shown that they were capable of perpetuating those values which favor the continuity of the country and which allow its specific character to be safeguarded. A point of encounter, Morocco has always opened itself to others throughout its history without betraying its own essential nature. Geography has endowed Morocco with an exceptional natural aperture, making it a crossroads for civilizations and a privileged witness to historical events. Dominating the western part of the Mediterranean a few kilometers from the European continent, on the principal axes that lead towards America or the East, firmly united to Africa, from earliest times Morocco has experienced the greatness and the vicissitudes inherent in its strategic position.

The limits that derive from its geographic position actually constitute an advantage. Coveted by many, both then and now, this position also favored national unity, the birth and development of what makes Morocco unique. It was enriched by this opening towards the outside world and the ensuing contacts, and it was this encounter which gave shape to its distinctive identity. To cite just one example: when the Romans settled in Volubilis, they adapted their architecture to the lie of the land and the pre-existing city, founded by Juba II, as well as to the ornamental motives dear to the people of that time. The result was the lovely city of Volubilis. While not completely Roman, it none the less bears witness to the greatness of its builders and their considerable adaptability. The reciprocal influences bore fruit and the adjustments involved are tokens of an unbroken continuous evolution from which both parts unquestionably benefitted. Another symbol: Islam. This religion rapidly conquered the heart of the Moroccans, who became its strenuous defenders. Their constant systematic commitment in defense of the Islamic faith in Morocco hardly needs mentioning. The resistance to foreign occupation in Tangiers, El Jadida, Essaouira, Agadir, Chechaouen... amply testify to this fact.

Moreover Muslim Morocco has always played an active part in spreading Islam. Ever since Okba Ibn Nafi reined in his horse before the Atlantic Ocean, the Moroccan people have always worked to overcome the obstacles that the sea placed to the advance of the territory of Islam. They took up Okba's torch and moved towards Europe. Tarik Ibn Ziyad crossed the Strait of Gibraltar with an army of eight thousand men and succeeded in converting the Spaniards en masse. He thrust as far as Poitiers. Later, numerous inhabitants of Africa and some of the Arab countries were persuaded by the Moroccans to embrace the faith of Islam and to reinforce the rank and file of Muslims. Still today the commitment of Morocco for the cause of Islam cannot be denied. Morocco was host to the first Islamic conference, which it promoted after the fire in the mosque of Jerusalem. One of the outcomes of this conference was the Islamic conference organization which nowadays is marked by its dynamism, its aspirations and its multiple initiatives.

On the other hand, in this fortress of Islam, the presence of the faith is manifested both in private and public life by the Moroccans and the outstanding position this religion at present occupies is the result of numerous centuries of history. Ever since the arrival of Idriss I on Moroccan soil and the founding of the Idrissid dynasty, Islam has become the keystone of the socio-political system. Neither the past, nor the present can be understood unless they are seen in this light.

When the founder of the Idrissid dynasty was assassinated by the Abbassids, what was it that stopped the Moroccans from taking back the power that had remained vacant? Idriss II had not yet been born and could not succeed his father until several years later. Loyal to the founder who was above all a descendent of the Prophet, and in respect of the commitment assumed with their oath of loyalty, the Moroccans saw to the education of the child who, at the age of eleven, was nominated successor to his father. As a result, the attachment to Islam and the capacity of the Moroccans to defend the faith guaranteed the continuity of power and the legitimacy of the sultans. This was the case with the Almoravids who introduced the Malikite rites into Morocco and which are still observed. And the same holds true for the title of Amir El Mouminine (commander of the faithful), used for the first time in Morocco by Yusuf ibn-Tashfin, and at present appearing in the constitution as the principal title of the head of State. In the period of the Almohad dynasty, the sultan Abd al-Mumin «founded the greatest empire of the west which ever existed» before taking on himself the title of Caliph and ordering that the prayers be recited in his name. All the greatness of the Merinids is bound to the holy war they fought and the religious monuments they built. Appealing to the religious sentiments of the Moroccans, the Saadians came to power, committing themselves with determination in the holy war (jihad). They freed numerous cities from foreign occupation. Ahmed al-Mansur spread Islam in Africa and reached as far as Timbuctoo. He strenuously opposed the Turks. The Alaouite dynasty was predestined to take up this task. Resistance against foreign occupation and the management of public affairs in conformity with the dogmas and the religious precepts are a recurrent feature in this dynasty. Moulay Ismail freed Tangiers from English occupation and took back Mehdia and Larache from the Spaniards. Sidi Mohammed ben-Abdallah did the same for El Jadid and Agadir, pushing the Spanish back into their Mediterranean strongholds. Moulay Sliman ensured the guardianship of his country by creating contrasts between the various powers. Still too young, Moulay Abd al-Aziz was incapable of opposing foreign expansionistic aims and the oulema (men of religion) preferred his brother Moulay Hafid. After signing the treaty of the protectorate imposed by France, Moulay Hafid abdicated and placed the power in the hands of his brother Moulay Yusuf. Some years later, in 1930, France mistakenly interpreted the rivalry between Arabs and Berbers and a dahir was promulgated which withdrew the latter from Islamic jurisdiction. Everywhere manifestations of protest took place and riots broke out against what was interpreted as an attempt at Christianization. In all the mosques the Moroccans repeated these words: «God, let us not be separated from our brothers». The resistance was organized and the signs of protest against the protectorate multiplied until independence was obtained. The Feast of the Throne celebrated first in 1934 to renew and confirm the act of loyalty which unites the sovereign to his people, became particularly meaningful in 1956. King Hassan II applied himself to constructing a modern state with adequate norms and institutions. This is why the constitution of Morocco is often compared to the one which France acquired in 1958. Despite the similarity of the text, an eminent place is reserved to Muslim public law. The old and the new each enrich the other.

In this domain, as in that of architecture, of music, of painting, of cinema, of theatre, of culture, of the culinary arts, of customs, the opening to the outside bowed to the needs of the continuity of the tradition. Naturally, as King Hassan II affirmed, «Morocco takes care not to live in the past. It only uses its past as a source from which to draw the great examples and teachings which can lead it towards the future» (cfr. Le Défi, p. 189 ff.).

Fez, medrassa al-Sahrij, the multi-colored fountain.

The Tour Hassan at night.

The majestic mausoleum dedicated to the glorious ▶
sovereign Mohammed V.

RABAT

Situated at the mouth of the Oued Bou Regreg, Rabat is the administrative and political capital of the Kingdom of Morocco, the main residence of His Majesty King Hassan II, the seat of the government and the foreign embassies.

The city is tranquil with a climate that is mild in winter and cooled in summer by the ocean breeze from the Atlantic. The monuments, the places of note, the numerous beaches, the broad boulevards, the modern quarters, the traffic and tourist infrastructures make it a pleasant city to visit where one lives well.

Archaeological discoveries have revealed the existence of a settlement dating at least to the 3rd century B.C. At the end of the 1st century B.C., Sala already enjoyed independence, as documented by coins with neo-Punic inscriptions. In then became a municipality with the name of Sala Colona, and

then rose to the rank of colony. At the fall of the Roman Empire, Sala became no more than a village. In the course of the 8th century the population was gradually converted to Islam. Two centuries later a fortified monastery (ribat) was built on the site of the present Riyad des Oudaias. The builders, orthodox Muslims, fought a holy war against the Berghouata who had adhered to the Kharijite heresy. The name of the city, Rabat, derives from this ribat.

Around 1146, the Almohad sultan Abd al-Mumin was attracted by the strategic position of Rabat. He began to transform the fortified monastery into a kasbah and added a palace in which he then frequently lived. This was where he concentrated his troops at the moment of departure and return from his campaigns in Spain. His grandson Abou Yusuf Yakub al-Mansur dreamt of moving the capital of

The Tour Hassan looks down on Rabat.

The Mausoleum of Mohammed V, built by the ▶ architect Vo Toan in line with the Moroccan architectural canons.

his kingdom there. He founded the Ribat Al Fath (ribat of victory) providing it with ramparts several kilometers long and with four monumental gates. He decided, without succeeding, to endow the new city with the greatest sanctuary in Islam, the Mosque of Al-Hasan. At his death only the imposing tower, known as Tour Hassan, had been completed. A period of decline then began for Ribat Al Fath. Leo Africanus narrates that at the middle of the 16th century the city had barely a hundred inhabited houses.

In the 17th century a great number of Andalusian refugees settled in Rabat. They built a new city which they surrounded with the Andalusian wall and the town came back to life. In 1627, a group of pirates founded the Republic of Bou Regreg. The capital of this state which lived off piracy was installed in the Kasbah of the Oudaias. The principal targets of the pirate attacks were Spain, Portugal, France and England. Negotiations enventually led to cooperation between these powers and the Republic.

In 1666, the Alaouites once more gained control of the city and despite reprisals against the pirates, they were unable to put a stop to their activity, which continued up to the late 19th century. In the meanwhile the sultan Sidi Mohammed ben-Abdallah attempted to create a new city within the Almohad city walls. Even though he was not completely successful, he is to be credited for having endowed Rabat with two skalas, seven mosques and a palace which housed the negotiations with France in 1845 and in 1846.

When the Protectorate was set up, Fez became the capital of the kingdom. The new city, whose center was initially the district of the Ocean, extends between the palace and the medina. It is a charming town. Modern town planning begun in 1915 fits marvelously into the historical surroundings and broad boulevards join the quarters. The ministry buildings are set on a height and surrounded by lovely gardens with magnificent fountains. The residential quarters cover a large part of the new city:

A view of the Bab Errouah.

The facade of the Royal Palace, late 19th century, ▶
and the royal Mosque Ahl Fès.

Hassan, Orangers, Agdal, Souissi. In the last twenty years, however, Rabat has been expanding in all directions. New quarters have been developed along the Atlantic coast as well as towards the interior on the Route de Zaërs and on the Route de Temara. The streets of the medina of Rabat cross at right angles in an extraordinarily perfect ground plan.

This pleasant district begins where Avenue Hassan II and Avenue Mohammed V meet. From here one can admire the imposing city wall built by the Andalusians. A few meters on is the famous Rue Souika, the principal artery of the medina. On either side of this bustling street, cafés, restaurants and grocery shops, clothing stores and boutiques selling crafts attract a numerous clientele. Further on, on the left, the Rue Sidi Fatah is a surprising oasis of tranquility. This is the street that leads to the Moulay El Mekki Mosque, built in 1907, with a portico characterized by its painted ceiling that runs across the street. Turning into Rue Souika, we can admire the mosque built by Moulay Sliman. After passing a dozen or so shops, a lovely Merinid foun-

tain, now transformed into a bookshop, comes into sight. This 14th-century monument, in the heart of the medina, in the work of the sultan Abu Faris Abd al-Azia (1366-1372). The great mosque facing it also contains various mementos of this dynasty. This is where the covered street of the Souk Es Sebbat begins, the district of the leather workers and jewellery makers, which leads into Rue des Consuls. With the Mellah behind us to the right, it is no easy task to make one's way through the lively Rue des Consuls, flanked by tiny shops of tailors, merchants of cloth and traditional garments, by great bazaars and some warehouses. From this street, where the residences of the accredited ambassadors to Morocco were for many decades, numerous small streets open off. They constitute the core of the residential quarter characterized by the white walls and an unusual calm. Here there are small mosques and zaouiya (seats of religious fraternities). The Rue des Consuls leads to the large Place Souk El Ghezel, the starting point of Avenue El Alou which leads to the gate of the same name. Skirting the city wall on the outside,

Panorama of Rabat.

one reaches Bab El Had, which literally means «Sunday Gate». Actually the name derives from the punishment, Had, sanctioned by Muslim law administered in Morocco and the heads of those condemned to death were exhibited over the gate. Two pentagonal towers jut out from the curtain wall on either side, making access practically impossible.

One can, if one desires, go from the Place Souk El Ghzel to the **Kasbah of the Oudaias** nearby, one of the most attractive spots in Rabat. The foundation of this fortified citadel with its lovely garden dates to the Almohad period. Subsequently it was restored and consolidated at various times. Moulay Rashid added the entire southern part in the 17th century. The polygonal tower seems to date to the period of the Hornacheros who sought shelter in the Kasbah during the struggle against the Andalusians of the Medina. A guard walk runs along the upper part of the wall, about ten meters high and 2.50 m thick. A large gateway in freestone, magnificently sculptured on both sides, face onto the Rue Jamaa. The gate is considered one of the gems of Almohad art. Rue Jamaa is the principal artery of the Oudaias and

some of the buildings which line it date back at least to the 12th century. The El Atiqua Mosque, built by the Merinid sultan Abd el-Mumin, is moreover the oldest in Rabat. In the vicinity, the platform of the old lighthouse offers a splendid panorama of the beach of Rabat, the mouth of the Bou Regreg and the Skala, further down, set as defense.

The Rue Laalami slopes down between white walls which hide noteworthy dwellings and leads to the tower of Pirates. From the top of the tower a panorama of Salé and the lower part of the Kasbah is to be had. Another road, the Rue Bazo, leads to the Café Maure situated on a terrace opposite the city of Salé, and from which one can admire the upper part of the Kasbah. A small door leads from the café to a garden squeezed in between the overgrown ramparts. A permanent exhibition of local costumes has been set up in a large hall at the foot of the bastions. Overlooking it all is a large tall square tower, once part of a 17th-century construction. It is now the seat of the **Musée des Arts Marocains**.

Leaving the Kasbah, on the boulevard that skirts the Bou Regreg is the Museum of Traditional Crafts, the

Rampe Sidi Maklouf and the square of the same name. The **Tour Hassan** is in the immediate vicinity. Its minaret appears in the distance and indicates the direction to take. The resemblance of this incompleted tower with the minaret of the Koutoubia and that of the mosque of Giralda is unmistakable. It is moreover easy to imagine how imposing this sanctuary must have been with its 360 stone columns, still now standing inside the enclosure. The square tower, 16.20 m. per side, is 44 m. high and was to have been twice as tall. Inside, a broad inclined ramp leads to the top with its splendid view of Rabat, Salé and Bou Regreg.

At the other extremity is the **mausoleum of Mohammed V**, together with a mosque and a museum. Built in 1971 by His Majesty King Hassan II in honor of his father, sultan Mohammed V, the liberator of the Kingdom, it is a masterpiece of Hispano-Moresque architecture and traditional Moroccan art. The decoration achieves the maximum of its expression and is a faithful reflection of the evolution of art in Morocco from ancient times on. Rom Landeau wrote that the mausoleum «unites the majesty and sobriety of Almohad art, entirely dedicated to religion, Merinid elegance and pomp, and the sense of grandeur of the Saadian and Alaouite dynasties».

A few kilometers from the mausoleum, outside the city walls, is **Chellah**, also surrounded by imposing ramparts. The site has a twofold historical significance. It is here that the Romans built the ancient city of Sala, even though no significant ruins have so far been uncovered. The excavations now in course have done little more than establish the existence of this city and give us an idea of its importance. The Merinid presence is much more evident in Chellah. A monumental gate flanked by two crenellated bastions leads to the **Merinid tombs**. A path leads to the various monuments, including the sanctuary surrounded by koubas. Near the tomb of Abu el-Hassan and the tomb of his bride Chems Eddoha is a mosque with magnificent decoration still extant on the minaret. Not far off can be seen the ruins of a zaouia, while all around is a flower garden irrigated

The Kasbah with the Bab Oudaia.

by the waters of the Spring of Canons where the sacred eels live.

Next to Chellah is the **Royal Palace**. The buildings occupy the site of a vast Mechouar (royal enclosure) laid out as a garden with fountains and broad boulevards. It includes a fine mosque known as Ahl Fès where the king recites Friday prayers and those for religious recurrences.

On leaving the Palace through a fine gate that opens onto a tree-shaded avenue, one can turn left and continue as far as the **gate** known as **Bab Errouah**. The construction dates to the 12th century. It is the best preserved and the most remarkable of the gates in the Almohad walls. The decoration and size recall the gateway of the Oudaias. Four vestibules inside have been transformed into an art gallery. To the right of the Royal Palace, opposite the Moulay Youssef Lycée, the **Assounna Mosque** rises up majestically. The largest mosque in Rabat, its minaret dominates the entire city. Built by Sidi Mohammed ben-Abdallah in the 18th century, this mosque has frequently been restored. Boulevard Mohammed V begins on the large open square in front of Djemaa Assounna. The boulevard is separated in the center by grassy flower beds, with three charming fountains, and at the sides are the central Railroad Station, the Court of Appeals, Parliament, the Post Office, the seat of the Bank of Morocco, cafés, restaurants, modern shops and cinemas. This avenue leads directly to the medina, where the visit to Rabat began, a symbol of the successful encounter between old and new, authentic and universal.

The gate of the 14th-century necropolis of Chellah.

The picturesque figure of a traditional water vender.

Panorama of Meknès.

MEKNÈS

Situated about 140 kilometers east of Rabat, Meknès is one of the imperial cities. Still today, as in the past, it holds its own against the competition of Fez barely 60 kilometers away.

The name is intimately bound to Moulay Ismail, the great Alaouite sultan. But the origins of the city go further back to the 10th century when the Meknassa tribe settled on the banks of the Oued Boufekrane founding Meknassa Zeitouna and Meknassa Taza. The Almoravid ibn-Tashfin took these two villages in 1066 and began to fortify them. Around 1145 the Almohad Abd al-Mumin occupied Meknassa. The arrival of the Merinids was a positive event. Abu Yusuf al Yakub had a new Kasbah and a great mosque built. Abu el Hassan had a zaouia built as well as a medrassa, finished under Abu Inan and named after him.

The 15th century for Meknassa was a period of crisis. Abu Zakariya, of the Wattasids, brought peace, then maintained by the Saadians.

In 1672, Moulay Ismail transformed Meknassa into a true marvel when, after his rise to power, he transferred the capital there. The instability the new cities of Fez and Marrakesh represented for the new sultan and the presence of the springs of the Zerhoun, the wealth of the hinterland, the vicinity of the great communication routes which crossed Morocco from west to east, were the principal reasons for this choice.

Moulay Ismail used all his means and energies to endow his capital with grandiose monuments. He enlisted an army of laborers, masons, plasterers and artisans, recruiting black slaves, prisoners and the inhabitants of the nearby villages and personally participating in the task.

The destruction of the Merinid Kasbah and most of the medina is another sign of the will and ambition of Moulay Ismail. On the land thus cleared he had kilometers and kilometers of ramparts and walls built, with majestic gates, granaries, stables, basins, mosques, gardens, palaces and kasbahs.

The decline of Meknès began with the death of

The entrance to the tomb of Moulay Ismail. *A courtyard of the tomb of Moulay Ismail.* ▶

Moulay Ismail. Other buildings were of course constructed, but the transferral of the capital of Fez and the earthquake of 1755 sorely tried the city.

Today Meknès rises at the center of an extremely rich region characterized by a flourishing agriculture. It dominates an undulating verdant landscape covered with olive groves and bathed by the Oued Boufekrane which separates the city into two distinct parts: the old city (medina) to the west, and the new city to the east.

Meknès is the center for the collection and distribution of the agricultural products of the region: wine, cereals, citrus fruits, olives, oil, etc. and a food industry has developed. Cement works, a textile factory and establishments for agricultural machinery provide considerable employment. Arts and crafts are flourishing: painting on wood, pottery and embroidery.

Meknès is also an excellent tourist town, with good infrastructures. The medina preserves and maintains the remembrance of its prestigious past. A fine view of the medina with its minarets rising skywards is to be had from the new town. Subsequently departing from the gate of Bab al-Hedim one can

begin the visit of this marvel. Place al-Hedim is situated at the center of the old town.

This rectangular square lies between the medina, the mellah and the imperial city. Late in the afternoon it is particularly lively with acrobats, storytellers and vendors. The market, to the west, is highly colorful. On the south, the most imposing and majestic of the city gates rises up: **Bab el Mansour el Aleuj**. Construction begun by Moulay Ismail was not terminated until after his death, in 1732. It takes its name from the architect who designed it. Completely covered with ceramics and green mosaic, the gate is dominated by arabesque tracery. On the right is another gate of the same period, smaller in size but extremely harmonious, known as the Bab an-Nour. On the opposite side of the square is a building called **Dar Jamai** which the vizier Jamai, in the service of the Alaouite sultan Moulay el Hassan (1873-1894), had built. The fountain decorated with mosaic was built in 1914. At present the palace is the seat of the **Museum of Moroccan Art**. The original architecture of this outstanding example of a bourgeois 19th-century residence is well preserved and the Andalusian garden is beautifully kept. On

The Bab el Mansour, the most important gateway in Meknès.

leaving the museum, the Rue Sekkakim leads to the Bab Barrima. In the vicinity are the districts of the Mellah and the Berrima, separated by an internal wall that was part of a circle of walls erected to protect the Kasbah. The Rue des Bezzarin skirts the ramparts of the old city up to the Bab el-Jedid. The square of the same name is surrounded by warehouses and shops. The Rue des Serrairia joins the Rue des Nejjarin where carpenters and other artisans are at work. The En Nejjarin Mosque is at the end of this street. The minaret is the work of Sidi Mohammed ben-Abdallah. The Kissaria El Dlala at one side is particularly lively. Six days out of seven carpets are sold at auction here. Next the Rue Souk Es Sebbat, completely covered with bamboo, full of shops of cloth merchants, clothing and footwear, leads to the **Pedrassa Bou Inania**. This lovely building has fine chased bronze doors. Construction was begun by Sultan Abu el Hassan and terminated by his son Abu Inan. Identified by its odd dome, it dates to the same period as its namesake in Fez. As in all medrassas, it includes a central courtyard with a shell-shaped basin, cells for students situated above a gallery, a prayer hall with a mihrab. The particularly refined decoration is in majolica, carved cedarwood and stucco.

Facing the medrassa in the **Great Mosque**, the most important religious monument in Meknès. Built in the Almoravid period, the mosque was probably restored by the Merinids in the 14th century. In the immediate vicinity is the Filada Medrassa built by Moulay Ismail in 1689. Further on is the Kissaria, an imposing cloth and carpet market. By following the Rue Karmouni, one can cross the medina from one end to the other. To be noted at this point are the **El Mansur Palace**, the **Er Zitoun Mosque** and the **Bab el Berdaine**, the northern gate of the old city. Seen from the outside, it is truly magnificent. The name derives from the cedarwood market which was held in the neighborhood. But it is worth our whiles, leaving the Kissaria, to take the Rue Dar Smerr which leads to the Place el-Hedim and makes it possible to visit the old imperial city. Through the gate known as Bab Mansour one reaches the vast Place Lalla Aouda which stretches out between the walls and the district of Dar al Kebira, of which only a few vestiges remain. According to historians, the palace consisted of a score of isolated pavilions. Tall square towers with green tile roofs rise up above the walls. Three circles of defensive walls surround Dar al Kebira: the external walls are consolidated on the northeast by powerful square towers; the central walls had a guard walk that ran along on high for their entire length; the inner walls were the shortest

*The Bab el Khemis, built at the end of the 17th century
for Moulay Ismail and a picture of the Bab an Nouar.*

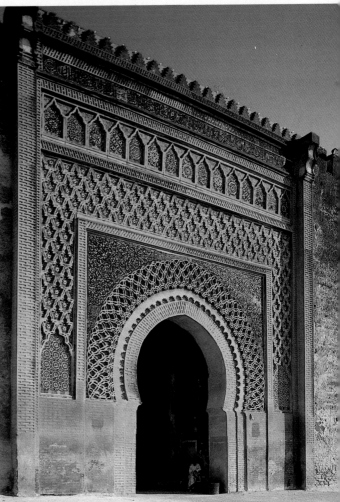

but also the highest. This complex included four
other symmetrically arranged pavilions and two
mosques, one of which was the Lalla Aouda
Mosque, visible from the square of the same name.
From here the gate known as Bab Filela leads to the
Qoubbet al-Khiyatin, a pavilion in which Moulay
Ismail received the foreign ambassadors. It is built
on a vaulted area spacious enough to hold thousands of prisoners or enormous quantities of
foodstuffs. On the opposite side of the square, the
old garden of the sultans has been transformed into
a golf course, striking in its greenery, for the beauty
and peace which reign there. In the vicinity, be sure
not to miss seeing the **mausoleum of Moulay Ismail**,
an occasion to pay homage to this great sultan. A few
meters away, the Bab al-Rih, the Gate of the Wind,
presents us with the beginning of a long vaulted
corridor formed of a series of arches supported on
heavy columns. At the end, one exits on a road
flanked by tall walls. On the right is hidden the **Dar
al-Makhzen**, the Imperial Palace, built in the 17th
century and opportunely restored. Behind the palace walls is the Mechouar, with a 19th-century gate.
On the left are the gardens of the Agricultural Insti-
tute (formerly Jenan Ben Halima), of which a fine
Andalusian garden still remains. Not far off is the
Heri or granary. Moulay Ismail made it large, and

Two pictures of the courtyard of the Bou Inania Medrassa.

immense vaulted silos were installed in a huge sub-terranean cubical construction. Above this were the warehouses set between large piers which supported the terrace roof. The thickness of the walls helps to preserve the supplies in the warehouse. The supply of water was ensured by wells that were about 40 meters deep. Water was brought up via a system of horse-drawn norias. This complex, which has now been restored, constitutes the **Dar el Ma**. Water for the irrigation of the gardens is collected in a basin four hectares large. Of the gigantic heri or granary (23 bays in all) nothing remains today but the piers joined by arches. After traversing the Bab el Aouda, a small street leads to the Dar el Beida. This is a vast palace built by Sidi Mohammed ben Abdallah at the end of the 18th century. The former residence of the sultan, it at present houses the Royal Military Academy. Further on is the quarter of the Jbabra with the old stables of Moulay Ismail which could hold up to 12,000 horses. At the center of this imposing structure is a domed hall used as the harness room. The

The entrance to the Dar Jamai, now Museum of
Moroccan Art.

great octagonal hall covered by a sixteen-sided
dome, still extant, was certainly part of this complex. Nearby the Jamaa Roua, built by Sidi
Mohammed ben Abdallah with a curious medrassa,
no longer used as such, leaning against it. Known as
the En Nouar Mosque, it overlooks the gate of the
same name and the Beni M'Hammad quarter.
Going round the Sultans' gardens, one returns to
Place El Hedim.
Other monuments and other sites of course also
merit mention and should be seen, including the
gates of Tizmi, El Khemis, Lalla Kadra, El Kari, Es
Siba, Bou Ameir, the mausoleum of Sidi Ben Aissa,
ancestor of the Aissaouas, the Kouba of Moulay
Ahmed El Ouazzani, the El Haboul garden as well as
the modern elegant buildings of the new city.
On the other hand, the region of Meknès is very
lovely, the rendezvous of charm and fascination.
Pleasant walks can be taken in and from the towns
of **El Hajeb**, **Azrou** or **Ifrane**.
El Hajeb on the way to Azrou is a pretty village

clinging to the mountain at an altitude of 1045 me-
ters with the remains of a 19th-century Kasbah.
Falls and springs abound in the immediate vicinity.
Not far distant, the route runs along the edge of a
plateau – the belvedere of Ito or the balcony of the
Tigrigra, with a magnificent view.
In **Azrou** it is possible to visit a Kasbah built by
Moulay Ismail in 1684 as well as a craft cooperative
famous for its collection of carpets.
Ifrane is an extremely modern town, founded in
1929 at an altitude of 1650 meters, a much sought
center in summer and a frequented winter sports
resort. From Azrou, the route which passes via the
Michlifen to Ifrane is highly recommended. From
Ifrane in direction Fez one can admire three lovely
lakes: Dayet Afourgah, Dayet Iffer and Dayet Al
Hachlaf.
The region of Meknès also includes historical sites
which must be visited, in particular the holy city of
Moulay Idriss Zerhoun and Volubilis.

The holy city of Moulay Idriss.

MOULAY IDRISS

Moulay Idriss is in the vicinity of Volubilis, about thirty kilometers from Meknès. It is one of the outstanding historical sites in Morocco for this is where the **tomb of Moulay Idriss**, the founder of the first Arab dynasty of Morocco, the Idrissids, is to be found.

Moulay Idriss, after whom the town is named, managed to flee from the Abbassids, whose rise to power his family had fiercely opposed. He found refuge in Morocco where as descendent of the Prophet he easily succeeded in obtaining the support of the Berbers. He was proclaimed imam on February 6th of the year 789 in Oualili. One after the other, all the principal tribes of the land swore loyalty to him. As he passed through the country he subjugated the other tribes. The Abbassids, envious of his popularity, in the end had him assassinated. Ever since, Oualili has become the goal of pilgrimages for Moroccans who come in great numbers throughout the year, in particular on the occasion of the great moussem or pilgrimage which is celebrated in August.

The city consists of two districts: Tasga and Khiber. The houses, with their green-tiled roofs, are set one above the other. The stepped alleys lead to the mausoleum and open onto the square of the souk with its typical animated shops. A modern cylindrical minaret, decorated with green tiles which reproduce verses from the Koran, contrasts with the predominant style of architecture without however diminishing the feeling of devotion and holiness that surrounds the town.

VOLUBILIS

Morocco's finest example of architecture in antiquity is Volubilis where the Romans built magnificent monuments. The origins of the city however date to much earlier times. Excavations begun in 1915 and still in course have revealed that the site was already inhabited in the Iron age and in the Carthaginian period. Ramparts dating to the period of Mauritania Tingitana and a Punic stele, which mentions the institution of a «suffectus» or magistrature, show that Volubilis possessed an urban layout prior to the 3rd century B.C.

The Romans introduced a new concept of urban organization in Morocco, bringing in the buildings to be found in all their provinces: city walls, forum, capitol, basilica. Actually, right at the beginning, they realized the problems involved in transplanting the orthogonal network typical of their cities. Since Volubilis already had its urban network and the lay of the land was particularly irregular, they had to adapt themselves to existing circumstances and attempted to improve the problems of circulation and the street facilities. The city had to be enlarged. A regular network of streets was envisioned in the northern and northeastern parts of the Moorish city that was gradually effectuated and terminated in 169 A.D. The Decumanus Maximus, a great artery between six and twenty meters wide, was put through this zone. The porticoes lining this street are barrel vaulted on the north and trabeated on the south so that the inhabitants could walk along covered sidewalks. The portico pilasters are decorated with Corinthian pilaster strips and capped by smooth-leafed capitals which support the entablature. A network of streets that was particularly efficient and exemplary for the times joins the various parts of the city. Water was brought in from a neighboring spring to the houses and public fountains via an aqueduct. Waste water and rain water ran together in a deep main drainage canal which followed the great artery and then emptied into the Oued Kroumane.

The Moorish walls, over 2.5 kilometers long, enclosed a surface of 40 hectares. As the city grew, the Romans enlarged them and added new city gates:

The triumphal arch in Volubilis.

Mosaics depicting dolphins and other animals in the House of Orpheus in Volubilis.

the one on the northeast called Tangier Gate opened on the Decumanus Maximus. It was comprised of pedestrian passageways on either side of a larger central opening for vehicles.

Various important public structures were built in Volubilis. The square **forum**, 1300 square meters large, was closed on the south by a tribune. This vast enclosed and paved area, situated at the point where the old and new quarters met, was the fulcrum of the political, administrative and religious life of the city. On one side it is flanked by a temple, on the other by a forensic basilica.

The **Capitoline temple**, built in honor of emperor Macrinus in 217 A.D., is set in an area 38 by 33 meters in size. The temple stood on a spacious paved and porticoed courtyard, of which various elements are still in existence. There was a rectangular altar at the foot of a monumental staircase in this courtyard, which led to the tetrastyle Capitoline temple with four columns on the facade magnificently restored and two columns behind.

The **basilica for judiciary audiences** is imposing and recalls the Severan basilica of Leptis Magna in

Libya. It was built at the beginning of the 2nd century A.D. Three steps and an external staricase lead up to it. Rectangular in shape, 42.20 m long and 22.30 m wide, it has a nave and ten side aisles, all separated by Corinthian columns. The nave, which is broader, is characterized by an apse at either end, entered through three openings with two columns. The apses were probably meant to be used as tribunals, while the adjacent rooms were used for the chancellory. A blind wall on the east separates the basilica from the curia, with which it communicated by means of an opening on the north and one on the south. The western facade with a central section composed of eight arcades flanked by two blind walls overlooks the forum.

Roman architecture is also distinguished for the beauty of its commemorative monuments, such as the **arch of Volubilis**, partially restored in 1931. It was built in 217 on a rectangular square where the city quarters converged and still bears an inscription which tells us that it was commissioned by the em-

The majestic ruins of the Basilica which was used as the court house.

The House of the Columns in Volubilis, 3rd century.

peror Aurelius Antoninus. Both the dedication and the first stone were placed thanks to the procurator Marcus Aurelus Sebastenus. The arch is decorated with a chariot drawn by six horses. It is an imposing monument built in local limestone, 19.28 m wide and 4.34 m deep, and consists of a single arch. Both facades are identical. Some of the details are singular and unquestionably foreign to the canons of Roman architecture. The same holds true for the niches adapted as fountains in each pier, preceded by two pedestals supporting Corinthian columns, which mark the borders of the basins in which the water from the fountains was collected.

Domestic architecture is greatly varied. Volubilis has houses built both for the popular classes and patrician houses that belonged to wealthy owners.

The more modest houses are grouped in the old southwestern quarter, built in pisè (clay masonry) and generally with only one or at the most two rooms. The dwellings in the residential quarters, with a peristyle, were derived from Hellenistic models and covered large areas. The walls, atriums, and pavements were sumptuously decorated giving the owners an opportunity to express their tastes and ideas and at the same time show off their wealth and prosperity. Two houses are particularly significant from this point of view: the **house of Orpheus**, which takes its name from the mosaic in the triclinium, is situated in the old quarter of Volubilis. It was frequently enlarged and embellished and contains all that is necessary for the family life and the activities of the owner and his family.

The **house with the mosaic of Venus** is more beautiful, larger and more harmonious. The entrance is spacious; the living quarters are arranged around a peristyle courtyard with a small garden. The walls are covered with interesting decorations. The ground floor, composed of eight rooms and seven corridors, is paved in mosaics with geometric motives and with mythological scenes of Greco-Roman repertory. The decoration and the fine *busts of Cato and Juba II* give us an idea of the luxury of this house. The Romans also built many structures for industrial and craft activities. There are traces of presses and bakeries. Oil presses were important in Volubilis because many olives were grown in the hinterland and have even been found in the rooms adjacent to some of the houses. Lastly, the **bathing establishments** were indispensable structures in the Roman cities and represented a certain degree of well-being. Those in Volubilis date to the Flavian period.

Other buildings in this lovely Roman city that merit mention include in particular the **house of the Ephebus**, so-called from the statue of an ephebus crowned with ivy found there in 1932. The ground plan, still visible today, evokes the beauty of the Roman dwelling of the Empire. The ephebus exhibited in the Archaeological Museum of Rabat shows us just how great the Roman sense of proportion was. The same can be said for the house known as that of the Labors of Hercules, the so-called palace of Gordian, the house of the Gold Coin and other monuments.

A **lapidary museum** has been installed near the entrance to the archaeological area of Volubilis. It contains numerous bases with inscriptions, capitals, fragments of sculpture, including the *Venus with a dolphin* and the *Bacchus* in white marble, both outstanding. Two mosaics exhibited on the wall depict a *head of Medusa* and an *allegory of the wind*. Those interested in decorative mosaics can see right there how well preserved some of them are. Geometric motives and arabesques reflect the favorite themes of the period.

The colors and hues are artfully combined. The loveliest mosaics are in the buildings on either side of the Decumanus Maximus.

The Decumanus Maximus and the ruins of the Forum.

Panorama of Fez.

A courtyard of the Attarine Medrassa, completed ▶
in 1325.

FEZ

Situated 60 kilometers from Meknès, Fez has various claims to nobility as one of the most prestigious cities in the Muslim world, for centuries a center for culture and religion, the melting pot of the Maghreb civilization. Moreover, Fez is the oldest of the imperial cities and the capital of the first Arab dynasty of Morocco.

The foundation of Fez dates back to the reign of Idriss I, when it was nothing but a modest Berber village (Medinet Fès) on the right bank of the Oued Fès, where the Andalusian quarter now stands.

Around the year 809, Idriss II, son of Idriss I, had the Idrissid capital built on the left bank of the Oued Fès. The city grew by leaps and bounds and quickly took shape. Refugees from Kairouan settled here while the Andalusians, expelled from Cordoba, peopled the right bank where Idriss I had built Medinet Fès. Thanks to the commitment, the competence and the harmony that was created between the peoples from Kairouan and the Andalusians, both cities flourished. Fez the became the cultural and religious center of all of Morocco and its architecture triumphed, with the construction of outstanding monuments, in particular mosques, built on both banks of the Oued Fès.

The Almoravids and the Almohads chose Marrakesh as their dynastic capital, but they never neglected Fez. During the Almoravid period, the two towns were enclosed in the same circuit of walls, creating Fès el-Bali (Old Fez). The reign of the Almohads was a fortunate period for the city, and culture and religion flourished and expanded together with a prosperous economy.

Under the Merinids Fez once more became the capital. The town was too small and a new urban center developed: Fès el-Jedid (New Fez). The new quarter

Partial view of the gate of Nehass and the facade of the Royal Palace.

was furnished with ramparts, a palace, a large mosque, a market, in other words with everything the new dynasty needed to affirm itself in the capital. Fès el-Bali however was not neglected and works were undertaken to make it more beautiful, including restoration. Fine medrassas, houses and magnificent palaces were built. Marble and majolica became the predominant decorative elements. The Qarawiyin Univeristy established itself as the center of culture and science. Trade was intensified.

When the Merinid dynasty drew to a close, Fez, exhausted by all these endeavors, went into a decline. The Saadians took over in 1544, but preferred Marrakesh as their capital. The Alaouites settled there before Moulay Ismail had decided to elevate Meknès to the rank of capital of his realm. For two centuries Fez was practically neglected. It was the Alaouite sultan Moulay Abdullah who relaunched

Fez which once more became the capital of the kingdom and remained such until the advent of the Protectorate. Throughout this long period, the city renewed its ties with its glorious past. The Alaouite sultans set about enlarging the city, preserving the historical patrimony and building new monuments. At the beginning of the 20th century a new city gradually began to develop south of Fès el-Bali and Fès el-Jedid. This modern city is quite extensive and at present is the administrative center. On the other hand it is the district which least reflects the characteristic features of Fez; its beauty, its secrets and its charm. In an attempt to fully comprehend Fez, the best way to begin is by visiting the medina. A striking panorama can be had from the summit of the Merinid tombs. The minarets seem to rise from a sea of white roofs framed by greenery and a chain of mountains.

An internal courtyard of the Bou Inania Medrassa.

The Bab Bou Jeloud and a detail of the great clock ▶
in the Bou Inania Medrassa.

Another splash of green consists of the roofs of the Zaouia of Moulay Idriss and the Qarawiyin lies at the heart of this sea. From here the city looks calm and peaceful. The unbroken wall of houses hides the streets and one wonders how the presumably numerous population can circulate and move within the city.

Very little remains of the 14th-century tombs. The road runs down near the Chardonnet fort and leads to Bab Guissa, the gate built in 1204 by the Almohad dynasty. A medrassa of the same name lies next to a mosque with a hall of the dead that dates to the 14th century. An adjacent gate leads to the Jamai Palace. This old late 19th-century aristocratic mansion was subsequently enlarged and transformed into a luxurious hotel. In the vicinity of the Bab Guissa is the Foundouk el-Ihoud of the old Hebrew quarter, replaced in the 18th century by the Mellah of Fès el-Jedid.

The entrance to Fès el-Bali is via the **Bab Bou Jeloud**, a particularly beautiful gate. Despite the style, it is quite recent and dates to 1913. With blue faience decoration on one side, and green on the other, the gate opens on two magnificent minarets.

One is that of the small mosque of Sidi Lezzaz, the other, with a more refined decoration dominates the **medrassa Bou Inania**, the largest and one of the best known and most important Merinid medrassas in Fez, built between 1350 and 1355 by sultan Abu Inan. It was at one and the same time a Koran school and a place of prayer. On entering one can admire its striking decoration. The door is in bronze and the steps, decorated in onyx and marble, lead to a wooden door that opens on a vast courtyard paved in marble, crossed by a small channel of flowing water from the Oued Fes. This courtyard with its finely decorated walls, paving, doors, windows and ceiling is sumptuous. The door of the study room is a masterpiece. The prayer hall has a mihrab and a mimbar carved throughout. Inside one can admire the beautiful stained glass, the capitals and the geometric ribbing of the ceiling. On leaving the medrassa, note the thirteen bronze chimes, set on a shelf. Above the chimes is a frieze in carved wood and stucco with thirteen tiny windows with traces of the mechanisms which set the chimes in motion. It is thought that these mechanisms were a clock, although from what is left, it is impossible to under-

Typical scene in the dyers' and tanners' quarter in Fez. Sheepskins and goatskins that have just been dyed are piled up on the terraces.

stand how it worked.

The Rue du Grand Talaa, the central artery of Fès el-Bali, joins the Bou Inania medrassa to the Attarine medrassa. Along the route a sequence of typical monuments and buildings can be admired: the Sidi Ahmed Tijani mosque, fountains, warehouses or caravanserais, guelsas (mosaic benches), the minaret decorated with glazed tiles of the Cherabline mosque, the souk of al-Attarine. Nearby the majestic **Attarine medrassa** rises up, built between 1323 and 1325 by the Merinid sultan Abu Said. The fact that it is smaller than the Bou Inania medrassa does not in the least mean that its beauty and precious decoration are inferior. The chased bronze doors open onto an interior of rare perfection: marbles, stuccoes, zellig, carved wood form a harmonious ensemble of great beauty.

Not far away is the **Qarawiyin**, one of the most important sites of Islam. Founded by Fatima el Fihria, it was originally (857) fairly small and was subsequently repeatedly enlarged, embellished and restored. In the year 933 it was transformed into a khotba mosque and in 956 it received a fine minaret. The Andalusian arists endowed it with all the elegance of Hispano-Moresque art. The part around the mihrab particularly strikes the eye. In 1135 the Almoravid sultan Ali ibn-Yusuf gave it its present size and form. It extends over an area of thousands of square meters and has fourteen large entranceways, and can contain up to two thousand worshippers. Today it is the only example of Almoravid building still in use. Subsequently the Almohads, the Merinids, the Saadians and the Alaouites left their marks on this monument which keeps the prestige of Morocco high throughout the world.

The medrassas al-Misbahiya, al-Seffarin and al-Cherratin were built around this great and ancient university.

To the west is the **Zaouia of Moulay Idriss**, a shrine which encloses the tomb of the founder of the city of Fez. Ever since the 15th century it has been a place of pilgrimage for the Moroccans.

The **Kissaria**, the commercial center of the city, stretches out between the zaouia and the Qarawiyin. A tangle of animated alleys makes it unique. Textiles and clothing can be bought here. The lanes near the zaouia have shops specialized in the sale of decor-

ated candles, lace, pottery and jewelry. A bit to one side, on the Place du Souk au Henné, the plant used for dying and for the treatment of hair, hands and feet is sold. Further on, **Place Ennejjarine** has a fine fountain decorated with mosaics, carved and painted wood and stucco. This square is surprising for the calm that reigns there, in contrast to the Place Seffarine with the din of the craftsmen creating their characteristic brass vessels. The trees and the elegantly decorated fountain make this square a cool spot, particularly appreciated in summer.

By turning into Rue Mechatine one reaches the tanners' quarter. The work can be observed from a terrace. The Oued Fès furnishes the water needed in tanning the skins.

The entrance to the Andalusian quarter is through the Bab Ftouh. Near the ramparts are the shops and kilns of the potters, as well as the shops of the craftsmen making the characteristic zellige or decorative tiles. In the immediate neighborhood is the **Mosque al-Andalus**, founded by the sister of Fatima al Fihria. It dates to the same period as the Qarawiyin. The imposing northern portal, decorated with zellige, and the carved wooden pent roof, are outstanding and make it a true masterpiece of Almohad art. Originally meant to be a simple oratory, the mosque was furnished with a minaret in 956 and enlarged by the Almohad sultan al-Nasser. The Merinids added a fine fountain (1307) and built the library (1415). Not far from the mosque is the **medrassa al-Sahrij**, so-called on account of the large basin at the center of a richly decorated courtyard. The teaching of the seven styles of recitation of the Koran have long made the nearby al-Sebayin Medrassa famous.

From Fès el-Bali, it is best to walk towards the Place des Alaouites to begin the discovery of Fès el-Jedid. Along the way one can take a side trip to the Dar-Batha which houses the **Museum of Moroccan Arts and Crafts**. Built at the end of the 19th century, the building is a noteworthy example of Hispano-Moresque architecture. It contains fine collections of representative art and craft objects from Fez and from the surrounding region. The archaeological section contains finds from the 12th century.

The Place des Alaouites is a vast square in front of the present entrance to the Royal Palace, Dar el Makhzen, surrounded by high walls and occupying an area of eighty hectares. Down below is the bustling Rue des Merinides. It runs through the Mellah or Jewish quarter, famous for its goldsmith shops. Bab Smarine is the real entrance to el-Jedid, a somewhat smaller and less picturesque quarter than Fès el-Bali. The gate with its great vaults opens on the large street flanked by numberless shops as well as the el-Hamra Mosque with a minaret dating to the 14th century on the right. The mosque of al-Azhar, built by the sultan Abu Inan, is a bit off to one side

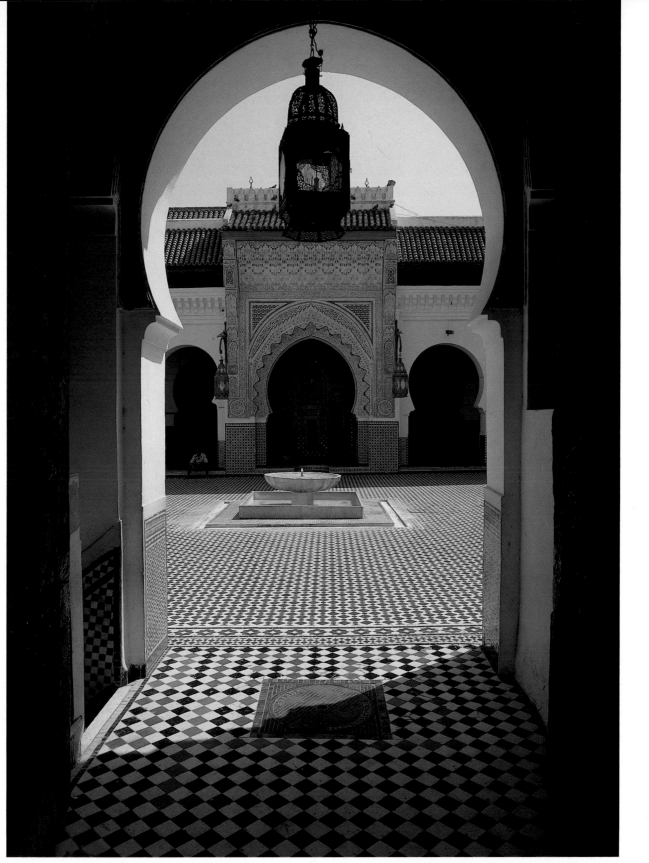

Place Ennajjarine with the glittering multi-colored fountain decorated with flowered mosaics and finely sculptured stone.

A courtyard of the imposing Qarawiyin Mosque, pride of Islam, venerated throughout the Maghreb. It is the sanctuary of sanctuaries for prayer and meditation.

Interior of the Al Sahrij Medrassa built between 1321 and 1323 and the magnificent portal of the Mosque al-Andalus.

A window of the Mosque al-Andalus.

and contains a carved portal, apparently from Andalusia.

After passing the Bab Dekaken, one enters the Petit Mechouar surrounded by high walls and situated above the Oued Fès. A gate opposite leads to the Moulay Abdallah quarter. To be noted is a noria built in 1287 to furnish the surrounding gardens with water. A bit further on is the great mosque near which is the *tomb of sultan Abu Inan*. Souks separate this monument from the mosque built by the Alaouite sultan Moulay Abdallah which encloses the mortal remains of the founder and of Moulay Yusuf in a kouba.

Near the Bab Dekaken, beyond the Petit Mechouar, the Bab es-Siba leads into the Vieux Mechouar. Late in the afternoon story-tellers, jugglers and dancers meet here, attracting a big crowd of onlookers. The Makina, on the west, was originally an arms manufactory and is currently in part occupied by a carpet factory. At the back of the Vieux Mechaouar the ruins of the old gate, **Bab Segma**, built at the time of the Merinid dynast, should be noted. It opens on the Cherarda Kasbah built by Moulay Rashid in 1670. It is now a hospital and includes the modern buildings of the Qarawiyin University.

The Borj Nord houses the **arms museum** with its noteworthy collection of weapons made or simply used in Morocco. From here one should return to the Merinid tombs close by for still another panorama of this magic city of Fez. A strange feeling takes hold of the visitor, a feeling that man can never unveil the secrets of the town, can never see or completely understand everything in this city so full of history and forged by time.

Two pictures of Place Mohammed V, the administrative center of Casablanca.

CASABLANCA

Situated halfway between Fez and Marrakesh, Casablanca is the largest city in the kingdom of Morocco. The other important cities are far behind both as regards population and economic importance. Over ten percent of the population of the country lives in this city which contains most of the country's industrial, financial and economic activities.

In the course of the last decades Casablanca has developed considerably. While the population numbered 250,000 at the beginning of the century, it currently counts over three million souls. The demographic growth has been on the increase ever since it was founded.

The precise origins of the city cannot be established for the site seems to have been inhabited in antiquity. A Carthaginian trading post probably existed on the site known as Anfa to the west of the present-day town. History was then to include the village among the small ports occasionally dedicated to piracy. From the time the Arabs arrived in

Morocco, Anfa prospered as the capital of the Berber kingdom of the Berghouta. The Almohad sultan Abd al-Mumin in the end broke the resistence offered by this tribe. Anfa then became a maritime port of call for merchant ships. Subsequently, due to its activities in trade and piracy, Anfa was subect to Portuguese reprisals. It was destroyed twice, in 1468 and in 1515. Sixty years later, the Portuguese rebuilt the city, furnishing it with fortifications and calling it Casa Branca. They stayed here for more than two centuries until the earthquake of 1755 and the unrelenting resistence of the neighboring tribes forced them to abandon the town.

Sidi Mohammed ben Abdallah, Alaouite sultan, undertook reconstruction of the town and gave it the Arab name of Dar el Beida. The Spanish, authorized to settle there at the end of the 18th century, rebaptized it Casablanca and this is the name by which the city is now known throughout the world. But at that time Casablanca was nothing but a village with less than 700 inhabitants (mid-19th cen-

The Habouss district, the old city of Casablanca and the mosque of the medina.

tury). Subsequently European tradesmen arrived and opened emporiums for buying grain and raw materials for the textile industry. Ships began to stop there and thus, gradually, a regular maritime traffic developed between Morocco and Europe. Merchants and Moroccan craftsmen arrived by the score and settled in what is now the old medina. England, Spain and France sent vice consuls to Casablanca. The population grew and at the beginning of the century numbered more than 20,000 inhabitants. Construction work on the modern port began in 1906. Casablanca then became the base for French penetration in Morocco. The massacre of nine port workers in 1907 and the blockade of the French consulate provided the pretext for military intervention.

In 1912 Lyautey decided to transform Casablanca into the principal port of Morocco and the principal seat for the European population. The development of the industrial, financial, commercial and port activities made Casablanca the economic capital of the country.

After World II, industry became particularly im-

portant, attracting massive investments of capital. The population, comprised of foreigners, Moroccans from other cities, in particular Fez, and above all peasants in search of work, continued to grow with a sustained rhythm.

The development of Casablanca, still on the upswing, is particularly favored by its geographical position at the center of Atlantic Morocco. The hinterland is rich, and Chaouia and Tadla have greatly contributed to the expansion of Casablanca. The site was not an obstacle to the enlargement of the urban center for the land is capable of sustaining an extremely dense urban agglomerate. Moreover history has helped in making Casablanca one of the most important economic centers in Africa. Thanks to its primary role in commerce it dominates the entire country. It is from here that imported products and manufactured goods are distributed throughout the kingdom. From the port of Casablanca the home products are shipped towards the other countries of the world. The principal banks, insurance companies and great companies all have a head office in this city.

A view of the Park of the Arab League which surrounds the city center.

Casablanca is moreover the industrial center of Morocco, with more than half of the country's factories. The textile industry is extremely varied and light and heavy industry are also represented.

Except for the residential quarters to the south and west, industries are to be found scattered throughout the city. Most of them however are in the quarter known as Roche Noires, near the port.

The site where the port is situated presented various problems. It is obviously artificial and jetties up to 18 meters deep and over three kilometers in extension had to be be built to protect it from the rollers which are particularly violent in winter. Since the coastal platform is sloping, draught for large tonnage had to be ensured by an embankment about 500 meters long. The result was a modern well-equipped port. The principal activity regards the exportation of phosphates, minerals, agricultural and craft products. Imports are no less important and comprised essentially of hydrocarbons, foodstuffs, equipment, chemical and metallurgic products. Passenger traffic as well as fishing are relatively unimportant. The unceasing activity which

characterizes its port has made Casablanca Morocco's principal point of aperture towards other countries and attracts numerous visitors.

Since it is a modern town the city naturally has no outstanding historical monuments. Even so it may be interesting to visit the medina, situated in the vicinity of the port,which surrounds the ramparts. The architecture of its houses and the labyrinth of lanes offer an interesting contrast with the modern part of the city. It buzzes with activity, in particular in the Rue du Commandant Provost, where the most varied array of articles and products in sold. Crafts are well represented and offer a permanent sampling of products from the regions of Morocco: carpets from Rabat, the Atlas and Sous, embroidery from Fez and Azemour, pottery from Salé and Safid; woodwork from Essaouira and Tatouan, Silver jewerly from Essaouira and Tatouan, silver jewelry from Tiznit, Taroudant and Tangiers. One can moreover admire the Skala and the Dar el Makhzen mosque, which was built in the 18th century, the kouba of Sidi ben Smara, the marabout of Sidi Belyout and the sanctuary of Sidi el-Kairouani. It is

Avenue des Forces Armées Royales, famous for its shops.

also possible to visit the church of Buenaventure built by the Spanish in 1891.

Near the old medina, a glassed-in dome with ecletic architecture indicates **Place Mohammed V**. This is the heart of the city, where the principal arteries cross, flanked by public buildings, shops, restaurants, hotels and cinemas. A passageway runs underneath making traffic easier. Boulevard Mohammed V and the pedestrian street Moulay Abdellah are particularly lively.

Opposite Place Mohammed V is another square famous for its musical fountain with jets of multicolored water, **Place des Nations Unies**, the loveliest zone in Casablanca. The buildings display a rational and original style: the Law Courts, seat of the Wilaya, dominated by a magnificent tower about 50 meters high, the main Post Office, the Municipal Theatre.

The Avenue Hassan II leads to the **Park of the Arab League** created at the beginning of the century and providing the city with an oasis of repose, diversion, and a place for promenades. The tall palms flanking the prospect of the boulevard create a restful environment which contrasts with the animation of

The Hassan II mosque.

the city. Other quarters of the city of interest include the new medina, built at the beginning of the century, with its souks, craftsmen, souvenir shops, the Mahakma or Moslem courthouse, traditional in its style of architecture and decoration, and the lovely Sidi Mohammed Ben Youssef Mosque. The residential quarter of Anfa with its lovely spacious villas climbing up the slope overlooking the coast and the seaside resort of Ain Diab along the coast with hotels, swimming pools, cafes, restaurants and night clubs. Nearby the aquarium of Casablanca contains fishes and other varieties from the marine world that come from all the seas of the globe.

A monument which symbolizes the solidarity, commitment, genius and devotion of the Moroccan people has been recently built right on the Atlantic coast, but much further west than the old medina: the **Hassan II mosque**, a jewel of modern architecture, situated in the heart of the most populated quarters of Casablanca. It prefigures the city's future, positively transforming the urban image. The medina will be rehabilitated, its monuments and walls restored, the commercial center enlarged and improved, large new roads opened, the coast will be newly structured, and the long beach of Ain Diab will receive still more specialized facilities. The entire city of Casablanca is preparing for a fundamental change that will make it not only the most modern city in Morocco, one of the most important African metropolises, but also and above all, one of the most beautiful cities of the world on the threshold of the 21st century.

The Hassan II mosque: details of the exterior and of the facade.

The Hassan II mosque: three views of the interior eith precious Venetian chandeliers and italian marble.

The white houses of Azemmour.

AZEMMOUR

Situated about 80 kilometers south of Casablanca, the city of Azemmour emanates a specifically Maghreb atmosphere. Built at the point where the Oued Oum er Rbia runs into the Atlantic Ocean, it was presumably known to the Carthaginians. For more than a century Azemmour was a particularly active Portuguese emporium and vestiges of that period are still extant. An imposing rampart of rare beauty surrounds this splendid city with its whitewashed houses and particularly interesting doors.

The bridge which crosses the Oued Oum offers a fine panorama of the town, characterized by the flourishing vegetation along the banks of the river.

For many years fishing, which flourished throughout the region, was the principal activity of the inhabitants. At present it has slacked off and even shad fishing has been jeopardized by the construction of the dam. The local craft of embroidery is also undergoing hard times. But agriculture is thriving, particularly tomatoes.

The potentialities in the field of tourism are being stressed. The beauty of the landscape and the charm of the medina go hand in hand with the mildness of the climate, both summer and winter, and the charm of the seaside resort of El Haouzia, situated only a few kilometers from Azemmour, on the road that leads to El Jadida.

The famous «Portuguese cisterns», enormous underground rooms, in El Jadida (formerly Mazagan).

The Bastion de l'Ange. ▶

EL JADIDA

The future in sight for El Jadida, about 90 kilometers southwest of Casablanca, is prodigious.

Its history and its position on the Atlantic coast made the city a famous tourist locality. The port of Jorf El Asfar, built in the immediate vicinity, has, in the past few years, made it an economic center of prime importance. The first documented historical mention of the city dates to the period of the Portuguese domination which began in 1502. Four years later it took the name of Mazagan. The Portuguese built fortifications and succeeded in maintaining their settlement for over two centuries despite the resistance of the population, sieges and attacks by the central power. Numerous vestiges of the Lusitanian citadel are still extant. The old city is also still surrounded by powerful ramparts, reinforced by four bastions, known as Holy Spirit, St. Anthony, St. Sebastian, and Angel. A canal runs between the walls of the first and the last of these bastions, a residue of the old moat which once surrounded the citadel. An underground cistern of the 16th century lies along the road that leads from the entrance of the citadel to the sea gate. It presumably was used as a storehouse until 1641 when it was transformed into a cistern to ensure a supply of water in case of siege. The vaults supported by 25 columns measure 34 meters per side. A circular opening, three and a half meters in diameter, at the top of one of the vaults furnishes a surprising play of light and shadow. This semi-obscurity is truly evocative.

It can be deduced from historical documents that Mazagan, at the time of Portuguese dominion, became the principal commercial emporium on the Atlantic seaboard, despite the Spanish parenthesis which lasted almost half a century.

The Alaouite sultan Sidi Mohammed ben Abdallah succeeded in liberating the city in 1769. But before abandoning it, the Portuguese evacuated the population and destroyed a great part of the fortifications. These had therefore to be reconstructed, and work was begun in 1815 by Abd al-Rahman.

A view of the Mosque of El Jadida.

A view of the city with the Bastion de l'Ange.

Even so the development of the inhabited area, which in the meantime had become El Jadida, did not really get under way until the end of the 19th century. During the French Protectorate El Jadida was once more called Mazagan and prospered and increased in size. After independence had been achieved, El Jadida went through a period of lethargy that lasted over a quarter of a century. Today it is once more a particularly dynamic city with an unprecedented development in all sectors. This transformation is in great part due to the infrastructures involving the railroad, the port, industry and culture, created in the city and surroundings. The hinterland constitutes an additional source of wealth for El Jadida. The plain of the Doukkala with the three dams that have been constructed on the Oued Oum er Rbia (Imfout, the most important, upstream, Daourate and Sidi Said Maachou) mean that the entire territory of the region can be irrigated. The production of grain has increased and other crops such as sugar beets and forage have been intensely developed. Grapes are traditionally grown in the plains and specifically on the scarp constituted by the interior meseta, both on small and large landed properties. Sometimes there is a rotation of wheat and barley which extend as far down as south of Sidi Bennour. The construction of the port of Jorf El Asfar a few kilometers from the city stimulated the growth of numerous industries, and an indus-

trial zone covering an area of 117 hectares has been created. With proper restoration, places of interest for tourists are coming back to life. A reduction of the population in the Portuguese city is considered a priority in the program of the public administration. Moreover, projects for safeguarding the city are also of a socio-economic nature and aim at offering the inhabitants a wholesome way of life with the creation of craft, commercial and tourist activities.
As a result the ruins have been cleared, the entrance streets have been enlarged, houses have been reclaimed and furnished with electricity and water. The streets and squares have been paved, in some cases with paving blocks or granite.
With an eye to increasing its tourist potentialities, plans for the installations of a fishing port and a harbor for pleasure crafts are at present under study. Once these have been realized, this seaside resort, endowed with an extremely mild climate and lovely beaches with fine sand, will merit its former name: Deauville du Maroc.
In its crafts, El Jadid has still another resource both for tourism and its economy. The specialized craftsmen working in brass are known throughout the land. The objects they make can be admired and bought in Place Sidi Mohammed ben Abdellah or Place Moulay Youssef crossed by the Rue Zerktouni, and which has become one of the liveliest quarters in the city.

53

The Kasbah of Boulaoune.

THE BOULAOUNE KASBAH

The name means «fortress of succour». This fortified castle is situated about fifty kilometers south of El Jadida, on the main road leading to Agadir. From its magnificent site it overlooks the majestic meanders of the Oum er-Rbia. From the Kasbah the splendid panorama embraces the whole river which runs through the plain of Doukkala.

This Kasbah was built in 1710 by the Alaouite sultan Moulay Ismail, as documented by an inscription on the architrave of the monumental gate.

The city walls enclose a rectangular area which is flanked by seven bastions and where the vestiges of the royal palace used by Moulay Ismail as road post can still be seen. There is also a mosque and some warehouses.

This Kasbah reflects the strategy adopted by the sovereign in his attempts to bring peace to the country and protect the population. Historians tell us that during his reign a woman could go from Oujda to Oued Noun without anyone asking her where she came from or where she was going. Many kasbahs were built under the incentive of Moulay Ismail. The most noteworthy are those of Adekhasan, on the northern border of the Atlas, of Agourai in the Middle Atlas, as well as the kasbah of Boulaoune.

Nowadays this kasbah and the surrounding region have become famous for a fine rosé wine known as «Gris de Boulaoune».

Various scenes in the potters' quarter in Safi and the castle overlooking the sea from which a splendid panorama can be had.

SAFI

Situated about halfway between Casablanca and Agadir, the city of Safi has always been bound to the rhythm of the Atlantic ocean which bathes its coast.

Presumably the name derives from the Berber «Assif» which means Oued, or river. Moreover, the city is crossed from east to west by the river now known as Oued Chaaba.

The date of its foundation cannot be determined with precision. Some take the origins back to the Carthaginians and others to even earlier times. In any case it appears that the city was built in the 6th century by the Berbers and was at the time no more than a small isolated center. In the 13th century activity began to thrive, sustained first by the Almohads and then by the Merinids. Around the second half of the 15th century, the Portuguese cast their eye on Safi and ended up by settling there. Resistance on the part of the indigenous populations gathered momentum and was organized, finally forcing the Portuguese to leave the city in 1541.

The Saadians, who had backed the populations during this struggle, took over the reins of the city. Safi and its port began to be intensively developed. The Alaouites, in particular sultan Sidi Mohammed ben-Abdallah, worked to create new centers of activity and to provide incentives for the port activities. This was when the aspect of Safi began to change and it acquired a dimension which it has maintained until today and which lies at the basis of its unique character.

It is first of all a city turned to the sea. Its activities center principally around the port. Fishing has always played an important role. Enormous schools of sardines are present thanks to the currents of cold water which bathe the coasts south of El Jadid in summer. As a result the industry for the conservation of fish has developed along the coast and employs much of the population.

On the other hand, the chemical industry has developed in Safi as well, where establishments for the

production of sulphuric acid and phosphoric acid
have already been active for many years. These
together with tinned fish represent a large percent-
age of Moroccan exports from the port of Safi.
But the city is famous above all for its crafts. The
potters' quarter is particularly lively. Although they
remain fainthful to the traditional techniques and
models, at times the craftsmen experiment with
more modern solutions and stubbornly attempt to
adjust their products to the current needs of the
clients.
On the level of tourism, Safi has resources of
cosiderable importance. The **Castle of the Sea**, now
restored, testifies to the Portuguese period. A magnificent view of the ocean, the port and the city is to
be had from the southwestern bastion. Nor must the
remains of a cathedral and the Moroccan fortress
called the Kechla within whose walls stands a noteworthy palace be forgotten. Moreover, Safi had
monuments built by the sultans of Morocco.

A view of the shoreline of Cap Beddouza.

CAP BEDDOUZA

Situated halfway between Oulidia and Safi, Cap Beddouza, formerly known as Cap Cantin, is a promontory on the western coat of Morocco.

Once, this elevated fragment of land stretching out into the Atlantic Ocean was one of the principal stopovers of the Carthaginian navigator Hanno, who dedicated a sanctuary to Poseidon in this tree-covered site in the midst of the lagunas full of canes around the 5th century B.C.

Nowadays little grows on Cap Beddouza, but the lovely beach offers a stupendous view over the Atlantic Ocean. Cap Beddouza is one of those unforgettable places which highlight the road along the Atlantic coast between El Jadida and Safi. With the antique Mazagan behind us, before us is the village of Moulay Abdellah, with its outstanding white Mosque and the ruins of the ribat of Tit. The road runs around Jorf El Asfar, offering splendid panoramas over the Atlantic Ocean as far as Oualidia. Overlooking the lagoon, **Oulidia** is a small seaside resort, the seat of a royal villa. It was founded in the period of the Saadian dynasty by the sultan el Oulad, who had the kasbah built as a defense of the entrance to the port. The vestiges of this kasbah, open to the public, add color to the ancient Air Laguna below. The itinerary continues on the road that, from Cap Beddouza on, winds along the edges of the cliffs which overlook the sea. After the beach of Lalla Fatma comes the promontory of Safi and Sidi Bousid which dominates the city of Safi.

ESSAOUIRA

Situated 130 kilometers from Safi, Essaouira is an attractive town. The islands in front of the city were inhabited as early as the 7th century B.C. The fragments of pottery found in situ bear witness to the fact that Phoenicians and Carthaginians stopped there. At the time of Juba II, Berber prince of Tingitana Mauritania, it was a flourishing center for the production of a purple dye used particularly by the Romans. In the 16th century, the Portuguese arrived and began fortifying the city which they called Mogador. It was in 1506 that the Portuguese king Manuel had an imposing fortress built there.

But the real history of Essaouira did not begin until the 18th century. In 1760 Sidi Mohammed ben Abdallah, fourth sultan of the Alaouite dynasty, attracted by its safe anchorage, constructed a port as well as a fort to protect the fleet. Historians say that another reason for the sultan's interest in Mogador was the fact that the insubordination and resistance of various great merchants and notables of Agadir and the surrounding regions could no longer be tolerated or remain unpunished. The sultan decided to compete with the city of Agadir and the first step in this strategy was the construction of the port. Activity was so intense and trade prospered to the point that the port of Agadir had to close. In an attempt to attract foreigners to Essaouira and convince the inhabitants to open up trading activities, numerous trade concessions were granted. The second step in this strategy was the construction of a new and beautiful city. Sidi Mohammed ben Abdallah wanted it to be larger, better equipped and organized than Agadir. He entrusted a French architect, Théodore Cornut, with the project and the beauty of Essaouira with its broad boulevards, orthogonal layout, citadels and monuments still surprises us today.

The platform of the Skala or fortification facing the sea offers an excellent panorama of this white city with its blue doors and shutters. It also becomes clear that the city was built on a peninsula.

An ever-growing number of visitors flock to the city, attracted by the town as well as the mild temperate climate throughout the year and the lovely beach

Essaouira, the Porte de la Marine built in 1769.

Above and on the facing page, the Skala of Essaouira, furnished with cannons; below, the Beffroi.

with its fine sand sloping towards the sea.

A visit of the city must include the port, the medina, the Skala, and the Jewish quarter or Mellah.

The entrance to the port is via the **Sea gate**, classical in style and built of stone. An inscription on the pediment tells us that the year of its construction was 1184 Hegira or 1769. The lively port is crowded with fishing boats and is also famous for its grilled sardines. When the fishermen return to port, there is an auction of fresh fish.

The medina is an extremely pleasant place. Specialized shops where all kinds of articles are sold line both sides of its broad streets. Avenue de l'Istiqlal leads to the market famous for the beauty of its porticoes. Avenue Mohammed Zerktouni, set on the same axis, leads to the mellah and Bab Doukkala. On the other side of the Avenue de l'Istiqlal (overlooking the port) a fine portico near the great mosque opens onto Avenue Oqba Ben Nafi, which is

actually a small square surrounded by walls.
The Skala of the Kasbah is a raised platform 200 meters long, protected by a crenellated wall. It is furnished with cannons decorated with heraldic emblems and imported from Spain and is dominated by a large square tower, from the top of which there is a splendid panorama over the Atlantic Ocean.
The chambers on the ground floor of the Kasbah house the best craftsmen of the city: experts in the production of admirable inlays in thuja wood, the real specialty of Essaouira, famous for the quality of the objects made: musical instruments, boxes, mirror frames, instrument handles, gun stocks, furniture such as tables, chairs, cabinets, side tables and book cases. The decoration consists of the typical geometric designs that belong to the repertory of Moroccan art. Thuja wood is inlaid with lime wood, mother of pearl, ebony and silver wire. These combinations make it possible to create a variety and

assortment of unheard-of beauty. Hundreds of hours of minute, precise and refined work are necessary to create these marvelous embroideries on wood. The Jewish quarter (Mellah) occupies a relatively large part of the city, witness to the importance of the Hebrew population that began settling here when Essaouira was founded. The Hebrews have actively contributed to the ecomic, social and cultural development of the city, with a conspicuous and fundamental contribution. The varying origins and the consequent amalgamation of the inhabitants are one of the reasons for Essaouira's unique character, reflected in the folk traditions and other artistic expressions. Still today many of Morocco's best-known figures in the world of theater, music, painting and the intellectuals come from Essaouira. The festival regularly held there in summer provides an idea of the city's artistic patrimony, exhibited on this occasion for the delight of all.

MARRAKESH

Marrakesh is one of the four imperial cities of Morocco. Capital of the Almoravid and Almohad dynsties, it was subsequently abandoned by the Merinids. The Saadians broght it back into vogue, but the Alaouites, while still concerned with its development and progress, preferred Fez, Meknès or Rabat as capital of the kingdom.

The city is important because of its geographical position where the north and south of the country converge, not far from the Sahara and the Atlantic Ocean. Numerous roads intersect in this city, to branch out towards Agadir, Casablanca, Fez or Meknès. Moreover, Marrakesh faces onto the mountain slope, opening itself towards the Sahara through the Tizi N'Test Pass and the Tizi N'Tichka.

But the city boasts an important history as well as the privilege of having given its name to the entire country. Presumably its foundation dates to 1070 by the Almoravid leader Abu Bakr who had the Kasbah (Qasr al-Hajer) built there. The ruins of this kasbah have been brought to light in the area north of what is now Koutoubia. As early as 1071 Yusuf ibn-Tashfin took possession of the city, endowing it among others with various monuments.

He strengthened his personal power to the detriment of his cousin Abu Bakr and extended his authority beyond the borders of Morocco as far as the Iberian peninsula. Marrakesh flourished thanks to economic relations with Spain. At his death he was succeeded by his son Ali ibn-Ysuf in 1106. It was he who had the famous Ibn Yusuf Mosque and a city wall built. He created a network of khettara or underground irrigation channels to ensure a supply of water. During his reign, Marrakesh assumed the aspect of true capital of an empire which extended from the Sahara to Ebro, from the Atlantic to Algiers. Trade prospered, crafts developed and intellectual and cultural life were intensified. No trace of all this remains. The Almohads did all they could to eliminate and cancel the traces of their predecessors, saving only the city wall, for its destruction would have meant the disappearance of the medina. Still now the old city is a reminder of the Almoravid civilization in Marrakesh. In 1147 Abd al-Mumin founded the Almoravid dynasty in Marrakesh, guaranteeing the city the role of capital of the king-

The Bab Agnaou, the most famous city gate, built in 1150.

The tombs of the Saadian sultans built during the ▶ reign of Sultan Ahmed al-Mansur.

dom. The Almoravid palace was replaced by the first Koutoubia, then by a second. He planned a vast garden with large reservoirs, His successor, Abu Yakub Yusuf, endowed the city with a new quarter and began to lay out a spacious garden. His son, Yakub al-Mansur, had a new kasbah built, including palaces, a kouba, bathing establishments, a kissaria, a hospital and even a race course.

During the reign of these three great sovereigns. Marrakesh returned to its past splendors. It became the center for commerce and culture. After the death of Yakub al-Mansur, a period of decline set in for the city, characterized by uprisings, revolts and sacking. In 1269 the Merinid sultan Abu Yusuf el Yakub returned as conqueror, but not long after, he transferred the capital to Fez. No important remains of the Merinid dynasty are to be found in Marrakesh.

The Saadians once more made Marrakesh their capital. The beginning of a great period in its history was responsible for numerous complexes which are the pride of the city, such as the Dar Si Said palace,

as well as the restoration of monuments. Many luxurious monuments were built and the traditional activities of the city came back to life and prospered.

The Alaouite sultans only occasionally lived in Marrakesh but they built the Bahia and Dar Si Said palaces as well as restoring much of the old town. The present king, Hassan II, is particularly fond of this city and frequently resides there. He has successfully undertaken projects for its embellishment and social and economical development and has endowed Marrakesh with installations and infrastructures of high quality. Its geographic position and its history make Marrakesh today one of the major tourist cities in Morocco. While the new city is not lacking in interest, the numerous monuments, witness to the splendor which fell to this city's lot, are to be seen above all in the medina. The best time for a visit goes from November to May. The sun is not quite as strong and the snow-capped mountains of the High Atlas rise up behind flourishing palmeraie. Carriages are a pleasant and economical way for

The great courtyard and two interiors of the Bahia
Palace, known as the «resplendent palace» and
built between 1894 and 1900.

A wall decoration in the Bahia Palace.

sight-seeing. One can begin with a visit of the center, in particular the **minaret of the Koutoubia**, to which the mosque of the same name owes its fame, characterized by an imposing architecture and decoration. The minaret, dating back to the Almohad dynasty, in form recalls the Tour Hassan in Rabat and the somewhat later Giralda in Seville. This splendid monument is the most perfect example of Hispano-Moresque art in the country. The architecture has skilfully wedded together stone, brickwork and cement. The harmonious external decoration differs on each side and consists of painted intonaco, floral and calligraphic ornaments, majolica, arabesques in relief and small arches. The minaret is all of 77 meters high and measures 13 meters per side. The external wall is 2.5 meters thick. The tower consists of six rooms one over the other with a slightly sloping ramp leading up to the top. Three great spheres of gilded copper, the largest of which measures two meters across, are set above the dome. This minaret is a distinctive feature of the horizon of Marrakesh, like the Eiffel Tower in Paris.

Two pictures of the al-Badi Palace, imposing monument constructed towards the end of the 16th century.

Not far off is **Place Djemaa-el Fna**, the greatest tourist attraction in town, situated between the medina and the Koutoubia. With its multiple manifestations, it is the center of city life and is constantly animated. Activity reaches its climax late in the afternoon when story-tellers, snake-charmers, dancers, acrobats, musicians, monkey tamers, sword swallowers, fire eaters and dentists are circled by curious and enthusiastic crowds. The square is surrounded by shops, cafés and restaurants which add color to the already highly colored atmosphere, where a variety of wares are on exhibit and the air is filled with the fragrance of the typical drinks and food offered to the passerby.

From here, it is best to move towards the **Bab Agnaou**, one of the city gates. Along the way, beyond the Koutoubia, is a whitewashed kouba which contains the tomb of the prestigious founder of Marrakesh, Yusuf ibn-Tashfin. The Bab Agnaou is surprisingly lovely, and is part of the Almohad city ramparts built by the sultan Abd al-Mumin in the year 1150. The gate opened onto the kasbah built by

Yakub al-Mansur. The richness and elegance of the structure and the decoration make this monument one of the outstanding examples of Maghreb military architecture. Once past the gate, on the right one can see the mosque of the Kasbah, known also as **el-Mansouria**, after the man who had it built. Restored by the Saadian sultan Moulay Abdullah and subsequently by the Alaouite sultan Sidi Mohammed ben Abdallah, a minaret of harmonious proportions rises over the building.

To the right of the mosque a path leads to the **Saadian tombs**. This necropolis dates to the 16th century. The Saadian prince Mohammed Esh-Sheik was buried here in 1557. Later Moulay Ahmed al-Mansur had it embellished and he and his successors were also buried here. The Alaouite sultan Moulay Ismail had an enclosure wall built which shut off access until 1917 and hid the place from sight. Only then could the splendid masterpiece of Muslim art once more be seen. A garden separates two mausoleums, each of which contains several rooms. The first has an interesting mihrab. The sec-

Two pictures of the Koutoubia Mosque with the famous minaret dating to the year 1190 and considered the emblem of Marrakesh.

ond, in the center, houses the **tomb of Ahmed al-Mansur**. Next to him repose his children and his grandson together with other members of the family. In the third room is the tomb of Lalla Messaouda, mother of sultan al-Mansur. Words cannot describe the elegance and sense of history that reign here in this climax of Hispano-Moorish achievement.

The Rue de la Kasbah leads to the Royal Palace through the Inner Mechouar, in communication with the **Agdal**. This garden park, of considerable size (3×1,5 km), dates back to the 12th century. All kinds of fruit trees have been planted here and particular attention has been paid to the olive trees which are plentiful in this paradise. Two basins make irrigation possible. It was Moulay Abd er-Rahman who had the Agdal garden set up and endowed it with an enclosing wall. Moulay Hasser reinforced the wall and added some gates. It is one of

these that leads to the **al-Badi**, a huge palace. The luxury, the splendor and the elegance of this dwelling of sultan Ahmed al-Mansur have been glorified by contemporary chroniclers. Decorated in marble, onyx and precious mosaics, the monument could not withstand the ravages of time. Moulay Ismail used some of the materials and fragments to build the palace of Meknès. Currently the Folklore Festival of Marrakesh is held at the end of May or in early June each year in the setting of the vestiges of the al-Badi Palace.

The Mellah, up to 1936 the largest Jewish quarter in Morocco, stretches out to the east of this palace. On the north rises the **Bahia Palace** built by the great vizier Ba Ahmed around the end of the 19th century. It is an outstanding example of residential architecture which covers about eight hectares of land. It consists of a sequence of apartments set around

A detail of the interior of the Ben Yusuf Medrassa, dating to the 15th century.

courtyards filled with trees and flowers. Each apartment is elegantly decorated. The gardens are admirable.

Rue Riad Zitoun el-Jedid leads to another lovely 19th-century dwelling, **Dar Si Said**, which probably belonged to the brother of Ba Ahmed. At present it houses the **Museum of Moroccan Arts** and contains collections of ancient carpets from the Upper Atlas, pottery from Safi, weapons, jewellery, marbles and stuccoes, as well as a collection of Saadian wood panelling, reconstructed ceremonial objects and ancient architectural fragments.

The visit to the old city and the souk can begin from the Place Djemaa el-Fna nearby. The medina is surprisingly animated. The quarter of the souks can be reached either from the Rue des Potiers or from the Rue des Epiciers. The gate at the end leads into the Souk Semmarin, occupied by textile merchants. In the vicinity, an alley flanked by apothecary shops leads to the Rahba Kedima which for a long time

was an important market for cereals and slaves. This square is surrounded by the wool souk and the sheepskin market. Next come the souk Zerbia and the jewelers' souk. In the immediate vicinity is the Kissaria or Qissariah where everything can be found; from modern products to craftwork. At this point the road narrows and leads to the artisans' souk.

Here one can see all kinds of craftsmen at work: leather artisans, makers of slippers or babouches, saddlers, workers in wood, cordmakers and those who fashion brass vessels. The dyers' souk is near the Ararines souk, and a visit is of particular interest. The skeins just dyed are hung to dry on long canes stretched from one side to the other of the street. It is an extremely colorful spectacle. The stepped alley then leads to the mosque and Al-Mouasin fountain. Another road leads to the Chouari souk and the Haddadin souk. Nearby is the 12th century **Kouba al-Baroudiyin**. The ribbed dome is strikingly beautiful. In the vicinity, the **Ali ibn-Yusuf mosque** has nothing left to show of its Almoravid origins despite restoration. The minaret is 40 meters high, rising up over the mosque and the Koran school nearby. This **medrassa** is one of the most noteworthy monuments of the medina of Marrakesh. Founded by the Merinid sultan Abu el Hassan in the middle of the 14th century, it was completely rebuilt by the Saadian sultan Moulay Abdullah, as witnessed by the inscriptions incised on the lintel and the capitals of the prayer hall. Entrance is through a long corridor. The spacious courtyard, paved in marble, has a large rectangular basin. The entrance to the prayer hall is flanked by two elegantly carved marble slabs. Under the arches is a magnificent marble ablutions basin, decorated with three tiers of floral motives, winged quadrupeds and heraldic eagles. The prayer hall is magnificent with its double row of marble columns, its finely carved mihrab, the dome and the tiny windows. The cells of the students on the upper floor overlook the courtyard and offer a fine view over the medina.

From this medrassa one returns to the Ali ibn-Yusuf mosque to reach, via Rue Baroudienne and Rue Amesfah, the fountain known as Chrib ou Chouf (drink and admire), decorated with a fine facade in carved wood. Rue Bab Taghazout leads to the mosque and medrassa of Sidi bel-Abbas. Both were built by the Saadian sultan Abu Fares in 1605. The adjacent mausoleum, built by Moulay Ismail is a prilgrimage site. It houses the **tomb of Sidi bel Abbas**, who lived in Marrakesh during the reign of Yakub al-Mansur, and whose devotion and wisdom were exemplary. He is also said to have achieved miracles which greatly impressed his contemporaries. Sidi bel Abbas is one of the seven patron saints of Marrakesh venerated by the Moroccans: Sidi Youssef, Cadi Ayad, Sidi bel Aggas, Sidi ben Sliman, Sidi Abd el-Aziz, Sidi el-Gheqouani and Sidi Essoheyli.

The road that leads to the Djemaa el-Fna runs along the zaouia of Sidi ben Sliman el-Jazouli, a charming building of Saadian date surrounded by various

The lower mechouar of the Royal Palace.

The pavilion in the Menara Gardens.

The principal entrance of the Royal Palace. ▶

pious institutions. In the 18th century Sidi Mohammed ibn-Abdullah restored the complex. In the immediate vicinity stands the mosque of Bab Doukkala, built around 1557 for Lalla Massaouda, mother of the Saadian sultan Ahmed al-Mansur. The **Sidi el Hassan** or **Ali fountain** is not far off. It has a basin 15 meters long and 5 meters wide and has three domes over it.

At this point the visit of the northern part of the city, including the souks, the monuments and numerous points worthy of interest, terminates at the Djemaa el-Fna. This by no means signifies that Marrakesh has revealed to the visitor all its wealth and secrets. Quite to the contrary! There are still many things to be seen – the splendid **Menara Gardens**, covered with olives. In its calm waters a central basin 200×150 meters in size reflects the pavilion with its green-tiled pyramidal roof built by Sidi Mohammed ben Abd er-Rahman and restored in the 19th cen-

tury. Still to be seen is the **new city of Gueliz** which stretches out to the northwest of the medina. It is outstanding for the modern aspect of its buildings which relate to the old city in their ochre color, typical of Marrakesh. Then mention must be made of the Majorelle Botanical Gardens, with a wealth of rare and exotic plants in the heart of the palmeraie which covers well over a thousand hectares and is one of the great attractions of this lovely southern capital. Then there is all the rest: the marvelous city gates (Bab Aghmat, Bab Ahmar, Bab Ighli, Bab Ksiba, Bab er-Robb, Bab Echcharia, Bab el-Jedid, Bab el-Makhzen, etc.); the mosques, the zaouia, the fountains and the souks.

The surroundings of Marrakesh also deserve to be mentioned: the villages of Tabeslouht, Amizmiz, Asni and Imlil, Mount Toubkal, which rises to 4165 meters, the valley of the Ourika and the ski resort of Oukaimden.

An evocative picture of the Ouzoud Falls.

THE OUZOUD FALLS

Situated in the Middle Atlas Region, 150 kilometers northwest of Marrakesh, the splendid falls of Ouzoud (110 m) are the highest in North Africa. It is a favorite site for the tourist and nature lover. From any angle, the cascade is overwhelming in its beauty.

Seen from below, the spectacle is enchanting. The water, apparently gushing from the sides, the vegetation on the cliff and the rays of the sun blend together into a phantasmagoria of colors. The spectacle is accompanied by a deafening but magnificent roar of the water, transformed into music as it swiftly flows along, a music which the mingling of the torrents as they cross and converge in the falls

amplifies. A circular lake temporarily collects the limpid pure water before it runs out into the Oued Ouzoud, the source of which is 3 kilometers upstream, and which then runs into the Oued el Abid, diluting its reddish waters.

Climbing back up the path that runs along the falls, the eye embraces the two successive levels of the cascade. From above one can see olives and tamerix and, in the distance, the majestic mountain peaks. It almost looks as if a human face had been carved on one of those rocks, while an opening in the center of a rocky cliff recalls the windows built by the Portuguese in the Middle Ages.

AGADIR

Situated 273 kilometers southwest of Marrakesh, Agadir is one of the loveliest cities in modern Morocco. Its story is that of one beginning after the other: after reaching the zenith of prosperity, a natural calamity or a political decision sent it on its way back down.

The name is derived from the Berber language and means, in the region of Souss and the High Atlas, a fortress, a warehouse, a silo or a fortified dwelling or even a bulwark or a kasbah. These constructions were generally built in elevated positions or in places that were hard to reach for reasons of safety and defence. They could be used either as dwellings or to store provisions; in particular crops, grain and oil. These reserves were set aside to be used in time of need, especially in case of war. But the Igoudar were often trading posts and caravan stopovers.

The city of Agadir has long served as regional capital for the provinces south of the Atlas. When in 1505 Joao Lopes Segueira built a rudimental fishing port in Agadir called Santa Cruz, the settlement served principally as a base for the Portuguese occupation of the Souss Valley.

The population revolted against the abuses perpetrated by these outsiders. After various years of struggle and resistance, the Portuguese were defeated and left in 1541. The construction of Agadir dates to this period. The city then became a flourishing trading center. Sugar cane, hides and gold from the Sudan were traded with products of European origin. When the Alaouite dynasty assumed power, the sultan Moulay Rashid went to

Panorama of Agadir.

The modern buildings of the Fiduciaire du Sud and the City Hall.

Agadir and exhorted the inhabitants to do all they could to develop the city and the region. In the middle of the 18th century an earthquake destroyed most of the city, and activity slowed up. The interest shown in Agadir and its port by the Europeans, in particular the Danes and the Dutch, together with the appearance in the region of groups that opposed the central power, engendered a reaction on the part of the sultan Sidi Mohammed ben Abdallah. He liberated the city in 1756 and a few years later had Essaouira and its port built, with disastrous consequences for Agadir. Activities in the port practically came to a standstill, while the caravans of the Sahara continued on to Marrakesh for supplies and to sell their wares. As time passed, Agadir once more recovered its role and position and during the reign of Moulay Sliman there was a remarkable comeback of the city whose reconstruction was successfully promoted by this sultan and by Moulay Hassan.

In 1913 the French navy attacked the city. It was occupied and transformed into a strategic stronghold, the point of departure for the submission and pacification of the entire region. Economy was blocked for over ten years and the port fell into leth-argy. Towards the end of the twenties, the economy slowly began to revive but it was not until the forties that capital and investments returned to Agadir. The entire region of the Souss profitted and agricultural crops were diversified. In the meanwhile fishing, preserving and transformation industries developed.

When it regained independence, Agadir once more had a chance to develop its potentialities which were duly identified and exploited. The city once more became the principal pole of development for southern Morocco, a role for which its geographic position at the point of convergence between north, south and west had ideally prepared it. The presence of this city was also important in opening up the surrounding regions. The port makes it possible to sell local products (minerals, fruit, vegetables, fish) and to import what the region needs.

On February 29, 1960 a violent earthquake destroyed 80 per cent of Agadir, with 15,000 dead. The city ceased to exist. Immediately after the disaster, exhorted by the voice of sultan Mohammed V, the Moroccans, defying nature, began to reconstruct Agadir. The sovereign announced that if fate had wanted the destruction of Agadir, the entire nation was in mourning, adding a phrase that was to become famous: «The reconstruction of Agadir will be the work of our will and our faith». This phrase, today documented by facts, is also written on a cement wall built to commemorate the commitment assumed by the sovereign and his people. The present king of Morocco, Hassan II, as hereditary prince at the time, had actively participated in the reconstruction of Agadir and had written in his book **Le Défi** (p: 131): «Our father's vow has been fulfilled. Even though it was not given him to see the new Agadir with the eyes of the living, his spirit floats over this city which, as the foreigner says, presents an admirable architectural unity... It is national solidarity which has made Agadir a flourishing city... Now it symbolizes for us the rebirth of Morocco and the fidelity of its people. Death and misfortune have mercilessly struck and it is with humble dignity that we can affirm that, thanks to God, they have been vanquished». Consequently the city once more stands on the route that through Tiznit, Sidi Ifni, Goulimine and Tarfaya, moves down southwards, towards the vast horizons of the refound native country.

And it is quite true that after its reconstruction Agadir is more beautiful, more active and dynamic, and therefore more important, than ever. Its tourist resources as well as its role as hinge between north and south (to which the recuperated Sahara provinces must be added) have been intensely developed.

At present Agadir has the first port for fishing in the kingdom. It provides employment for many and has led to the creation of industries for the preservation and transformation of the catch.

Crafts prosper and agriculture has been rationalized in the plain of Souss. The mild winter climate is a factor that is favorable for the growing of early season crops and citrus fruits. It also favors the vineyards, apricots and plums. Tourism is fast developing and Agadir is now the principal tourist site in the entire country. Twenty-three percent of the tourists who visit Morocco stay in Agadir. The city does of course have many peerless resources. Kilometers of lovely beaches stretch along an enchanting ocean with warm transparent waters. The soft brilliant sun makes the climate temperate throughout

A typical example of modern architecture on Avenue du Prince Moulay Abdallah.

Two pictures of the coast with the bathing establishments.

the year and luxurious hotels in which to rest, have fun and practice sports line the entire coast of the town.

The city is worthy of interest. The streets glitters with the thousand colors of the wares and products on exhibit. Traditional and modern are crossed and blended in perfect symbiosis: architecture, costumes, music, languages...

In addition to the buildings of exemplary beauty which are part of the reconstructed city (post office, town hall, law courts), mention must be made of the Kasbah, whose walls seem to resist the wear of time and which do not belie the name attributed to the city. It dominates the valley covered with green vegetation as well as the majestic massifs of the Anti-Atlas and the immense blue expanses of the Atlantic.

Outside the city and in the surroundings, numerous localities of historical and naturalistic interest increase the tourist resources of Agadir, the point of departure for delightful excursions. Besides the val-

ley of the Souss, trips can be made to the predesert region of Goulimine, to the imperial city of Taroudant, to the legendary cities of Tafraout and Tiznit. Exciting and sometimes unexpected discoveries can be made in the markets held regularly in these localities. Crafts are particularly creative and original. Jewellery, weapons and carpets perpetuate an ancient traditional art. In **Goulimine**, an outstanding trading center on the threshold of the desert, the camel market every Saturday gives one the chance to meet the «Blue Men», the nomads of the Sahara thus called because of the blue clothing they wear which tinges their skins blue. They have been coming to this city for time immemorable. Their women are famous for the dance known as of the «guedra» or of the pot. This gestural expression is known throughout the world. The representation of this ancient dance which makes the most of the natural feminine grace attracts an enthusiastic crowd at the national folklore festival in Marrakesh in May, or at the Meeting of the African Folk Arts in

Two views of the port of Agadir with the fishing nets.

July in Agadir. The dancer, on her knees, girates to the rhythm of a large drum and exhibits herself in a mimicry which expresses a vast range of feelings.
In the field of folk arts, the region of Agadir has other attractions in addition to the «guedra». Other forms of artistic expression (story-telling, organization of festivals and moussem, dance and music) compete and firmly maintain their original features. The Souss is the kingdom of the Rouai. Each tribe, in line with tradition, has a rais who is at the same time poet, composer, musician, story-teller and head of his company. Their songs furnish precious information on the history of those tribes and on their daily life. As far as dance is concerned, Souss is celebrated for the *Ahwachs*. These are dances of various types and diverse form. They all however begin with a simple song, interpreted as a solo in a high key by the head of the company. After which the drum chimes in, announcing the dance, executed with the utmost discipline.

The blue spring and the walls which surround Tiznit.

TIZNIT

The name of this city evokes above all a legend. It is said to have been founded by a woman, Fatma Tiznit. Some see her as a precursor of feminism, others as a sinner who, fed up with her family, fled with her lover and went to live near a spring which like the city still today bears her name. Naturally Fatma Tiznit in the end repented and decided to live an exemplary pious life. Numerous devotees joined her and after her death a mausoleum was erected in her honor. The city of Tiznit was founded around this monument over fifteen centuries ago.

Historical sources set the origins of the city in more recent times. The Alaouite sultan Moulay el-Hassan had the city built for military purposes. This is why there are imposing fortifications in pisé around the city, with bastions which reach up to the palm groves and the gardens.

Today it is an outstanding tourist locality. The visitor is overcome by a sense of bewilderment on market days as he admires the lovely jewellery in solid silver which has made the region famous.

In particular, one should see the famous and precious fibulas of Tiznit, an antique example of which is on exhibit in the Museum Dar Jamai in Meknès. It is a real masterpiece in silver set with stones, and with traces of niello characterized by a harmonious composition of lines, geometric forms and colors.

TAFRAOUT

Situated 198 kilometers from Agadir and reached via Tiznit, the city of Tafraout is known for the enchanting beauty of its landscape, the dynamic character of its inhabitants and for the marvelous localities around it.

Tafraout is a real paradise. In the heart of a picturesque valley of the Upper Atlas region, it is framed and protected by a crown of mountains in pink granite. The cubical houses are set against the multitude of rocks in their chaotic shapes from which they sometimes seem to emerge. The landscape, with its palm groves, makes it unbelievably beautiful. In the second half of February the variety of colors is astonishing when the ephimeral color of the blossoming almond trees is added. Other trees and crops, such as olives, oranges, lemons, figs, barley, corn and vegetables heighten this phantasmagoric effect even further.

But the principal activity of the Ammeln tribes which populate the enchanting valley of Tafraout is no longer solely agriculture. The scarsity and irregularity of rain, together with the poverty of the soil, mean uncertain harvests. The inhabitants are often forced to emigrate. The men leave their native land for several years to look for work elsewheres in Morocco; sometimes abroad, so they can save some money and return home. Their predisposition to trade is legendary and we find them almost everywhere in the cities of Morocco. Their grocery shops or stores is all they live for. Costs of management and what they need to survive are reduced to a minimum. They work all week long, opening early in the morning and closing late at night. All kinds of staples are found in their shops and when they have

The picturesque houses of Tafraout.

to or want to go back home a brother or other relative takes over and can in turn show just how good he is. This tradition has left positive marks on Tafraout. Economy bound to commerce is the principal source of investments on which numerous local activities depend and which together with tourism, guarantee the progressive development of this lovely region.

In the immediate vicinity of Tafraout is the picturesque village of Agard Oudad, set hard up against a rock that culminates in a curious conical form and is called «the finger» by the inhabitants of the zone. On the left, the piste of Ighrem follows the relief of this mountainous region and crosses the Tizi Mlil Pass (1650 m altitude) at the foot of the village of Idikel. A few kilometers on anothers piste leads to Ait Melloul, via Ait Baha and Ait Biougra. Still further on , the administrative center of Ait Abdel-lah precedes Azoura, where the circus of Idaou Zekri, consisting of curiously shaped rocks, can be admired. On a ridge stands a Berber fortress. Continuing in direction of Taroudant, below is the village of Ighrem. It is a fortified village, inhabited by the Idabu Kensou tribe, known for the elegance of their crafts, mostly daggers in chased silver, rifles decorated with marquetry, powder horns and vases. Continuing along the same road, one can visit Soul es Sebt of the Indouzal, the ruins of the kasbah of Freija and Tiout, which rises up on the left with a group of villages, a kasbah and a palm grove.

Departing from Tafraout, the road of the Ait Baha offers a marvelous view over the valley of the Ammeln, with villages clinging to the sides of the Jbel Lkest (2370 m). As far as Taguenza the landscape is enchanting. The olive groves and almond trees offer a surprising and picturesque spectacle.

A typical village clinging to the mountain side.

In the opposite direction, the road leads to the village of Oumensat, in the midst of gardens, from which the valley and the surrounding mountains can be admired. The road continues like this up to Agadir.

From this lovely and busy city, we advise you to pass via Tiznit to reach Tafraout. The highway is better and outstanding discoveries can be made. South of Tiznit, the road crosses Assaka and climbs to the lower wooded slopes of the Anti Atlas, following the valley of the Oued Tazerouait. At this point the Anti Atlas reveals its charm. It consists of a vast convexity of land aligned in a southwest-northeast direction. It culminates with Jbel Aklim (2331 m). At the center, erosion has brought granite and schist rocks to the surface. An intricate network of oueds, dry through most of the year, runs through this morphological complex, leaving deep gorges in the limestone mass.

On the right of the road, the piste of 4 kilometers leading to the **village of Iligh** begins. Formerly capital of the Tazeroualt, Iligh is also a center of the political, cultural and commercial history of Morocco. Between the 16th and the 19th centuries, the descendents of Sidi Ahmed ou Moussa (whose marabout can be visited) founded a small independent kingdom, detaching themselves from the central power. The only remains of this capital built in 1623 are a few koubas in which the founders of the dynasty are buried.

Returning to the main road, the pass of Kerdous can be seen passing over a mountain chain at a height of 1100 meters before crossing through the villages of Tizourhan, Arba N'Trafout and Affecha Wadaq, the last of which is famous for the decoration of the houses, in the immediate vicinity of Tafraout.

The 13th-century walls of Taroudant.

TAROUDANT

In the lovely valley of the Souss, Taroudant appears like a splendid immense garden. The entire city lies inside the walls which extend for kilometers and are over six meters high in some points. The land around the crenellated walls is covered with olive and orange groves, bananas.

The origins of the city go far back and extant documents mention it as early as the year 1030. At that time it was the capital of an independent principality, conquered by the Almoravids and which prospered anew under the Almohads before submitting to the Merinids. After various years of autonomy, Taroudant became an important operative base against the Portuguese who had settled in Agadir and naturally became the capital of the Saadian kingdom of Mohammed esh-Sheik. Throughout this dynasty, the city flourished. As the capital of Souss, its fortunes soared. In 1687 the sultan Moulay Ismail laid siege to the city and the consequent decline of Agadir and its port activities wiped out Taroudant's role.

Today the city is a stopover on the southwest routes. Agriculture in the region has been improved but Taroudant's age-old aspect and the beauty of the surrounding landscape have been left intact.

The souks are particularly lively and crowded. It is here that one can find chased silver jewellery set with stones, daggers, carpets, sheepskins, dates from the oases nearby and even the famous orange blossom essence.

The surroundings of Taroudant are a vast oasis at the center of the valley of the Souss. The gardens inside the city walls continue on the outside, even occasionally hiding the villages scattered here and there under the dense foliage of the trees. Further on is a plain where argan trees still grow. At the foot of the mountains, the outlets of the valley are characterized by a myriad of oases. The most important is the **oasis of Tiout**, southeast of Taroudant.

The luxurious vegetation contrasts with the surrounding desert. Above a kasbah which dominates this oasis the waters of a spring gush forth and irri-

One of the entrances to the town of Taroudant and an
artistically decorated door of the Hotel Salam.

gate the palm grove.
On the road to Marrakesh lies the Tizin-Test, whose
peak rises up to 2100 meters. From this point one
can enjoy a stupendous panorama of an
otherworldly landscape. Then the road slopes down
gradually in the midst of this lovely landscape to the
kasbah Tagoundaft, perched on the top of a hill like
an eagle's eyrie. Beyond this fortress, built in 1860,
and along the road leading to the deep valley of the
Oued Nefis, one can visit the famous ruins of **Tin
Mal**, ancient city built by Ibn Toumart in the 11th
century, a few years before the Almohad dynasty
rose to power. Only a few fragments of wall and
some of the well-preserved arches of the oldest
mosque in Morocco have resisted the ravages of
time and according to a legend, the whims of the
women.
The outstanding architecture of this religious edifice
certainly served as model for the Koutoubia of
Marrakesh, presumably rebuilt by the successor of
Ibn Toumart.

Two partial views of the Kasbah of Taliouine.

TALIOUINE

Taliouine is situated at an altitude of 930 meters on the transverse route that joins Agadir to Ouarzazate, seventy kilometers from Taroudant. It is surrounded by almond groves and dominated by a height on which stand various ruins. It has a beautiful Kasbah.

Between Taroudant and Taliouine lies the village of Aoulouz. The ford over the Oued Sous is more or less passable, depending on the season. From Aoulouz one can reach Ansel, through the Tizi N'Melloul pass, 2506 meters altitude, on the rainshed of the Jbel Siroua.

Along this piste one can meet the descendents of the Ouzguita tribe, famous for the carpets known as *Habel*, the textiles and their burnooses.

The road to Taliouine passes through Agadir Touksous and rises on the wooded slopes up to a pass at 1050 meters, from which the stupendous valley of the Oued Souss can be seen.

After passing Taliouine, the road leads to the Tizi N'Taghatin pass (1886 m) on the watershed ridge between the valley of the Souss and the valley of the Draa. On these heights lives the tribe of the Sektana.

Not far off, the Tizi Irhsane pass (1650 m) leads to the village of Tasenakht. The local crafts cooperative exhibits objects that have become famous for the richness, harmony and elegance of the work. Continuing along the same road, one reaches the Tizi N'Bachkoum pass at 1700 meters, with a marvelous view of the Jbel Siroua and the Anti Atlas before continuing for Ouarzazate.

OUARZAZATE

Situated at the crossoroads of the routes to Dades, Draa, Souss and Marrakesh, Ouarzazate has become one of the best-known tourist centers in Morocco.
Founded in 1928 as a military garrison, the city then became the administrative center of the region of Draa, after which it rose to capital of a vast and beautiful province and with a considerable historical background.

The city itself attracts visitors for its craft center, where Berber pottery and, in particular, the Ouzguita carpets are sold.
A few kilometers from Ouarzazate, on the road to Marrakesh, the **kasbah of Tiffoultoute**, built in pale ochre pisé, rises at an altitude of 1160 meters. In the past its inhabitants were a threat both for Makhzen and for Ouarzazate and the surrounding zones. Today the kasbah is no more than an attraction for tourists who go there to admire the magnificent panorama over the valley through which the Oued Ouarzazate runs.
Another interesting monument is the **Taourirt Kasbah**, nearer to Ouarzazate, which can be reached via the road of Boumalen du Dades.
Once the residence of the Pasha of Marrakesh, this kasbah built in pisé is nowadays urgently in need of restoration. The buildings were mainly military in function and the whole is a sort of fortified city, with numberless lanes. From the terrace of the kasbah one can admire the mountains, the lake formed by the Mansour ed-Dahbi dam, the oases and the enchanting Draa Valley.

A fascinating view of the Kasbah of Ouarzazate.

Two panoramic views of the enchanting Draa Valley with its palm groves and small Berber villages

THE DRAA VALLEY

The upper reaches of the river Draa run in a northwest-south direction, separating the Anti Atlas from the Jbel Sargho. The course of the river has dug imposing gorges in the rocks which then widen out in a stupendous valley, which extends from Ouarzazate up to M'Hamid. The particulary arid soil aborbs a part of the waters which eventually flow into the Atlantic Ocean.

The Draa furnishes innumerable oases with water and runs through the charming Draa valley, over 200 kilometers long. Flourishing cultures grow in the shade of figs, pomegranates and palms, lending color to the landscape. Here and there buildings in pisé known as ksour and villages of various sizes are to be met with.

Forty-two kilometers from Ouarzazate, at the foot of th black rocks of the Jebel Tiffermine, is the **village of Ait Saoun** surrounded by groves of almond trees which stand out against the pale earth typical for the zone. The meanders of the river Draa wend their way through a land with various levels. Before reaching Agdz, a visit to the falls of the upper reaches of the Draa can be made as well as to the vast palmeraies on the bank of the river a few kilometers away. It is an oasis covered not only with palms, but also with fruit trees, oleanders and fields of wheat. The variety of the crops and the color contrasts are striking.

Agdz is the administrative center of the Mezguita oasis, one of the five oases in the valley of Draa. The village came into being on the right bank of the river on highway n. 31 which connects Marrakesh with Zagora, about 65 kilometers southeast of Ouarzazate. Built at the foot of the Jbel Kissane, Agdz developed slowly and even now still has its red plastered houses, making it look decidedly rural despite the presence of administrative, social and economic structures. Facing it, on a small height set on the

other bank of the Draa, is the **kasbah of Tamnougalt**, formerly capital of the Mezguita. This kasbah surprises both for the decoration as well as the interior arrangement of the buildings it encloses. On the slopes of the Jbel Kissane various ksour are set one after the other, flanking the green line which marks the sinuous course of the river. Two groups of buildings stand along this route, whose modern aspect contrasts with the traditional architecture of Agdz. The first, surrounded by the palmeraies of the Mezguita and the Tinsouline, is known as Tansikht, while the second, called Rbat Tinzouline, is famous for its ksar and for the lively market on Mondays. Subsequently the road and the river pass through the Azlag Gorge and continue towards neighboring Zagora.

This is the principal administrative center of the Draa valley. It was founded probably in the 11th century, as witnessed by the ruins of an Almoravid fortress at the summit and the foot of Jbel Zagora. However, piles of stones known as «tumuli» scattered throughout the Draa Valley, the remains of tombs of earlier periods, lead to the supposition that this zone was heavily populated prior to Almoravid domination.

Afterwards, the city played an important role in the history of Morocco. From a political point of view, the region of Zagora is the cradle of the Saadian dynasty. On an economic level, in the past it was an important stopping place for caravans on the route to Timbuctoo.

At present Zagora is a major tourist center. From Jbel Zagora the panorama is magnificent and embraces at one and the same time the palm grove, the desert which surrounds it on all sides almost as if to swallow it, and the bare mass of Jbel Sargho.

Just outside the city, in the midst of the sand dunes stands the ksar of Amzrou. Gradually the horizon flattens out up to the great desert.

In the vicinity, the **village of Tamgrout** is an ancient religious center of considerable importance, famous for the zaouia of the Nassiriyin, a religious brotherhood, whose influence extended to the entire Draa Valley, the Dades, Souss and the Anti Atlas. Still today one can admire the rich *library*, collected in the 17th century by Abou Abdallah Mohammed

Bennacer with precious manuscripts, in particular illuminated Korans on gazelle hide, the oldest of which date to the 13th century.

From Zagora a fascinating route continues on to the oasis of Ktaoua, to Tagounit and finally M'Hamid. Here the Draa curves out and, after crossing the last palm groves, the waters of the river lose themselves in the vast stretches of sand, attempting to find their way to the Atlantic. This is where the vast arid desert plateau begins, and the vegetation marks the end of the Draa Valley.

In this valley the river is the principal vector for communication, life and development. The aridity of the climate makes agriculture impossible outside the oases. The outlet to the south and the High Atlas mountains bar the way to the humid north winds, so that the valley is exposed only to the hot winds of the south. As a result, rainfall is very scarse, while temperatures go very high.

The population in the valley is mixed. The first occupants were Haratin and Jews, later joined by the Arab tribes who conquered it. Still today the different traditions and ethnic types testify to these varied origins. Naturally the various historical vicissitudes to which the region was exposed ended up by gradually bringing the inhabitants together despite diversity of origin and religious faith but even so each group succeeded in preserving its own unique nature and traditions.

Agriculture in the valley is highly varied and characterized by archaic and extremely complex techniques. The gardens, often tiny and enclosed in pisé walls, are irrigated by «seguias» which bring in the water from the derivations of the oud. The rare wells of the region are still exploited according to ancient methods. The land in the fields is hoed. Just about everything is grown, depending on the season, but grain and vegetables predominate. Every oasis produces cereals in autumn (wheat or barley) and in spring (maize). There are also orchards of fruit trees and palms.

Animal husbandry and crafts constitute complementary activities for the population.

This life style is subject to innumerable transformations and mutations. The construction of the El Mansour Eddahbi Dam on the Draa river made it necessary to reconsider and even abandon some of the traditional methods of irrigation and agriculture. The land system is in urgent need of redefinition and development of the valley runs the risk of being penalized and shackled. At this point, the population would be forced to emigrate or collect in the villages scattered through the valley.

A fortress in the Draa Valley.　　　　　　　　　　　　　　*The hauting landscape of the Dades Valley.*

THE DADES VALLEY

The Dades Valley occupies the entire zone that separates the High Atlas from the mountains of the Sargho and the Ougnate. It runs along the southern slopes of the High Atlas, with peaks over 4000 meters high and snow capped up to and after June. This valley is included in the immediate neighborhood of Ouarzazate and Boumalen du Dades.

The Oued Dades which begins in the massif of the Mgoun flows through the valley and makes it possible to cultivate the adjoining lands throughout the year. The presence of water and the fertility of the soil have attracted various peoples as far back as antiquity. The Haratin seem to have settled here in neolithic times. Around the 17th century, the foundation of the zaouia of Sidi ben Nadji on the plain of Skoura encouraged the construction of fortified buildings or ksour and kasbahs. They multiplied for reasons of security and they became the typical type of dwelling in the life of the valley.

The population, with its various ethnic backgrounds, fused in the course of the centuries into the present Ahl Dades. The valley has preserved its traditional beauty and charm, particularly to be appreciated in spring and early summer. Agriculture is flourishing, with rose gardens, fruit trees with an abundance of apricots, peaches, almonds.

The Dades Valley is also celebrated for its kasbahs and the famous **Route des Kasbahs** runs along the entire length of its 200 kilometers. These innumerable constructions bear witness, on the one hand, to the struggles for supremacy that took place here, and on the other, to the importance of the region economically and strategically and its historical role as a communication node. These magnificent monuments keep the architectural features of the Berber tribes of southern Morocco intact. The principal dwelling centers of the oases and the valleys consist of fortified buildings with a prevalence of oriental and pre-Islamic Mediterranean influences in their architecture. Most of these kasbahs stand on steep heights, seemingly isolated and inaccessible as they dominate the valley. They were all built according to a single model and differ only in the various ornamental motive in unbaked brick. Often the decor-

97

The Kasbah of Ait Arbi.

Panoramic views of the Dades Valley ▶

ation is not purposely sought for but simply a result of the size of the kasbah. To tell the truth at a certain height it is difficult to use the typical pisé because of the weight of the wet earth which is its basis. The walls are therefore completed with adobe bricks, easier to transport and handle. Their form and size provided the masons with specific geometric forms which dictated the decoration of the facade. These buildings generally have two floors and are surrounded by high walls, reinforced at the corners by decorated towers which stress the defensive character of the kasbah. Dwellings, storerooms and warehouses set around various courtyards were grouped together in the ksour or fortified buildings. They were created to guarantee survival and defend the inhabitants. Inside, life is subject to a precise hierarchic order, based on social rank and economic conditions. Naturally the more well-to-do live in imposing larger kasbahs than do the others. The community buildings with wells, mosque, places for assembly and cemetery, are to be found within the ksar.

The visit to the Dades Valley begins with the fertile **oasis of Skoura** with its splendid palmeraie. Here there are charming villages and kasbahs with decorated towers. Particularly interesting are the kasbahs of Ameridil, el Kebbaba, Dar Aichil, Dar Ait Sidi el Mat and Dar Ait Sous. The Marabout granary of Sidi M'Barek o Ali, in the vicinity of Skoura, is famous for the dome of the kouba. Further on is the large village of the Mgouna situated at the mouth of the Oued Mgoun, at the center of an oasis where

A Kasbah in the Dades Valley.

The majestic Skoura Kasbah in the Dades Valley and the fantastic landscape of the Dades river at night

almond and apricot trees, pomegranates and other fruit trees grow rather than palms. Small roses known as «Baldi» grow in hedges and perfume the air. The flowers picked at the beginning of spring are used to make the rose water (attar) for which the region is famous and which is produced in the village in the rooms of a kasbah. This essence is widely used in Morocco. The Festival of Roses represents the climax of this harvest. The village is unusually animated and songs and dances with their unforgettable rhythms go on all night long up until dawn, a fantastic spectacle in an extraordinary atmosphere.

Another important administrative center in the valley is **Boumalen du Dades**. As at El Kelaa des Mgouna, palms are not grown here. The village is famous for the Wednesday market which is held in-side a vast enclosure in the lower part. A magnificent panorama along the green banks of the river begins at Boumalen. A mountain road leads to the spectacular and famous Dades Gorge. Thousands of centuries of erosion were required to sculpture the rock, giving it its present form and color. The cliffs that overhang this gorge are marvelous, the rocks varying in color from red to malva. Nearby are innumerable neat gardens.

South of Boumalen, the Jbel Sargho is situated on the extension of the Anti Atlas on the other side of the Draa valley. Further on, the ksar of Imiter and Timatrouine offer an interesting stopover thanks to their kasbahs along the route that leads to the lovely city of Tinerhir.

*Two pictures of the Kasbah of Tinerhir immersed i
green*

TINERHIR

Situated between the Tafilalet and the Draa Valley, Tinerhir is a true gem of architecture and surroundings. Built on terraces at the foot of a luxurious palm grove on which the windows of the houses in pisé open, it is a pleasant city to visit. Through its architecture the inhabitants call attention to the beauty and uniqueness of their villages. The kasbah dominates the dwellings, the palm grove and the surrounding countryside.

The weekly market takes place on Monday in a festive air and offers the opportunity to admire the outstanding objects of local crafts up for sale.

About fifteen kilometers away is the **Todra Gorge**, set in the midst of a fairy-tale landscape. The rocky steep walls in some places are 300 meters high. The

Oued Todrha flows through this deep cleft and i used to irrigate the almond trees. On the left, th spring at the base of the cliff attracts numerous visi tors. It is believed to have therapeutic properties fo barren women.

Moving upstream along the oud, numerous tiny vil lages are encountered here and there with a type o dwelling all their own. The walls are without win dows and the light enters from an internal courtyar used for various purposes.

This archaic type of architecture serves to keep ou the elements and the summer heat. It also permit the family to live in privacy, away from the pryin, eyes and curiosity of «strangers».

The ancient gate of the city of Rissani and a modern entrance.

THE TAFILALET

The region of Tafilalet lies at the southeast borders of Morocco, and played a pre-eminent role in the history of the country. The ancient Sijilmassa witnessed the birth of the dynasty of the Alaouites in 1640. The present king, Hassan II, is a direct descendent of Moulay esh-Sherif, the first sultan and founder of the dynasty. For many centuries Tafilalet has also been an important trading center. The principal gateway to the Sahara, it was the site of cultural exchange between the north and the deep south. Gold, spices and slaves passed through here on their way to the Sudan and Guinea.

Currently Tafilalet can be considered a tourist site of fine quality. Oases harmoniously mingle with the dense palm groves and the ksour, of which there are more than a hundred. The color contrasts lend a magical air to the landscape, enhanced by the surrounding mountains. The chain of the High Atlas, with peaks that are over 3000 meters high and which form a natural boundary of great beauty, is continued by the pre-Sahara reliefs which consist of semi-arid uplands at the gate of the desert. This diversity and coexistence results in an average yearly

An old man drying dates.

temperature of 19° C. Even so great differences in temperature exist in the mountain zones and in the desert uplands, between summer and winter, and even between day and night.

The Tafilalet is famed for its tourist zones. Three localities that merit particular mention are **Arfoud**, **Rissani**, and the **Ziz Valley**.

Arfoud is the point of departure for excursions in the Tafilalet region. The city is situated on the outskirts of the palm grove of Tizimi and Tafilalet which extend as far as the eye can see between the Oued Ziz and the Oued Rheris. One of the major oases in the region is to be found here and both it and the city bear the same name: Jbel Afroud. The numerous sand dunes around the oasis are used in curing rheumatism. Three kilometers away, the military site of Bordj Est offers a splendid panorama of the palm grove, the surrounding desert and the piste which leads to Taouz. There are numerous Ksour at Arfoud, in particular that of the Hbibat and that of the Chiahna. Deposits of lead abound in the region. The hardworking sober population lives from agriculture and trade.

On the way to **Rissani** one can visit the ksar of Tingheras with a fine view of the Tafilalet oasis, before crossing the site where Sijilmassa once stood. Only ruins remain today of the ancient capital of the kingdom built on the caravan route in the 8th century.

Today Rissani has become an important center. It is pleasant to amble through the streets so charged with meaning. The lively market, which furnishes a good picture of the traditions and culture of the peoples of Rissani and the surrounding region, is held three times a week. The ksar of Abouam, in the market square, bears witness to the economical, commercial and historical importance of the city. As the name indicates, the ksar was a permanent market for trade and negotiations.

The **mausoleum of Moulay Rashid**, founder of the Alaouite dynasty, is not far from Rissani. Destroyed when the Oued Ziz flooded, it was rebuilt in 1955 by the sultan Mohammed V. The sacred enclosure includes a rather spacious courtyard and a patio which leads to the funeral hall decorated with mosaics. Behind the mausoleum stand the ruins of Abbar ksar and, a little further on, the ruins of the Oulad Abd el Halim ksar. It is a marvelous edifice which, despite its present state of deterioration, is the most interesting building of this type in all of Tafilalet, with the admirable bastions, the towers and the monumental entrance to the kasbah.

The last thing to see is the **Ziz Valley** which has always been the gem of tourism in Tafilalet. The green zone is astounding and marvelous in the midst of the surrounding mountain landscape. The waters of the Oued Ziz gently flow through to irrigate the fertile palm-covered banks. The color and structure of the ksour scattered through the valley make them seem part of the rocky landscape. The Hassan Addakhil Da was built between 1968 and 1971 to regulate the flow of the river and guarantee the prosperity of the valley, safeguarding it from calamity. In this magical landscape it forms an artificial lake which makes this region, already so well endowed by nature and the hand of man, even more attractive for the tourist. Mention must also be made of the size of the region, the variety of mountain reliefs, the climate and the people, as well as the wealth of crafts, the numerous historical sites and monuments, the originality of the markets and the holidays, such as the moussem, which are regularly held.

The infrastructures are up to par. The highways are good and connect the localities of the region with the north of the country. There is plenty of drinking water. Of particular note are the tourist facilities which are rapidly increasing. Over 150 hectares have been set aside and prepared for the tourist projects to be realized in the coming years.

Two views of the Ziz Valley, irrigated by the river and with a wealth of palm groves.

The mosque of the city.

LAAYOUNE

For the Moroccans Laayoune is more than just a city. Its name is synonymous with the «Green March» and symbolizes the unity of the kingdom, so long dreamed of. Moreover, the projects so successfully carried out from 1976 on in the reclaimed Saharan provinces are a clear sign that Morocco is on the way to progress and prosperity in peace.

Situated 600 kilometers south of Agadir, Laayoune has innumerable resources which make it a desirable tourist center, at one and the same time a beach resort and a desert site. The contrast of the deserted stony rather monotonous uplands with the Atlantic Ocean which bathes the city is striking. The cold currents of the Canaries (situated opposite Laayoune) mitigate the aridity of the climate and make a sojourn here truly pleasant.

Hotel facilities are outstanding, modern and well balanced. Excursions in the surroundings take the tourist to a completely different world where sand dunes stretch out for miles, or give him the chance to discover infinite coasts.

The same can be said of the Naylat beach, 20 kilometers further north, or the beach of Foum el-Oued, the same distance away on the south coast.

The port and the stretch of shoreline of Tangiers called Avenue d'Espagne.

TANGIERS

Bathed by the Mediterranean and the Atlantic Ocean, Tangiers is distinguished by its history and its geographic position at the point where Europe and Africa meet.

The origins of the city go far back in time and legend has it that it was founded by Antaeus, son of Neptune and the Earth. Hercules gave Tinge, Antaeus' daughter, to his son as bride, after having suffocated her father and separated Africa from Europe with a single blow. The city was thus called Tingis. Subsequently Phoenicians and Carthaginians settled here, creating a trading port and a flourishing colony. When Carthage fell, Tingis first became a Roman colony dependent on the Spanish province, then capital of Mauretania Tingitana.

In the 5th century A.D., it was occupied by the Vandals for over a century. Under Justinian, the liberated city became part of the Byzantine empire. At the end of the 7th century it was occupied by the Arab armies. Moussa ibn-Noceir was particularly interested in the strategic position of the city. In the year 711 troops under the command of Tarik ibn-Ziyad left from Tangiers to conquer Spain. From then on, up to the Portuguese siege of 1437, various Moroccan dynasties, the Omayyads of Spain, the Fatimids and, subsequently, the Tunisian Hafsidi all laid their eye on the city. As a result Tangiers was constantly involved in the vicissitudes that characterized the story of North Africa in that period.

In 1471 the Portuguese returned to Tangiers as conquerors and occupied it for a century. As a result of alliances between the ruling houses of Europe, it became Spanish between 1578 and 1640, then once more fell under Portuguese dominion before passing to the English as the dowry of a Portuguese princess who married Charles II of England in 1661. From 1662 on it was permanently occupied by the English.

All the Portuguese churches, except one, were destroyed. Surrounded by fortifications, Tangiers' out-

Two views of the marvelous beach of Tangiers.

look for the future was bright as part of the possessions of the British crown, but the English lacked the time to carry out this project.

In 1678 Moulay Ismail laid siege to the city for five years. In 1684 the English, short of water, abandoned Tangiers destroying all they could. A new page in the history of the city had been turned with the liberation and the return to its homeland. Moulay Ismail successfully began reconstruction and reorganization of the town. On the site of the only Portuguese church the English had left standing he had the mosque of the Kasbah built, with an octagonal polychrome minaret. Under the reign of Moulay Sliman, Tangiers was the only city where diplomats accredited at the sultan's court were allowed to live. Naturally this was a cautionary measure. At that time Morocco was a land on which the expansionist aims of Europe converged with its numerous opposing rivalries. Signs of threats to Moroccan sovereignty were already in the air and they were to be confirmed with the passage of time. In 1912 the protectorate was imposed. Tangiers and the surrounding area became an international zone regulated by a statute in 1923. The city developed with a rhythm inconceivable in other parts of Morocco. In a quarter of a century it became a commercial center of international standing. The free port attracted investments en masse. The European colony which settled there was no longer composed solely of the wealthy businessmen, bankers and industrialists. Smuggling flourished to the point where the city was transformed into the «capital of ouverture, quick gains and easy pleasures», in the definition of Michel Rouzé.

When Morocco gained independence, Tangiers ceased to be subject to international law and once more became a city like the others in the country. Even so its historical patrimony is still very much there and its position gives it a unique character of its own. Present day Tangiers is the result of these two factors, opportunely balanced, and already on its way to a radiant future.

The important sites, monuments and districts preserve the traces and the mementos of the eventful history of the city. A complete panorama of this hospitable and at the same time familiar city can be had from Place de la Kasbah or the spacious terrace at the end of Boulevard Pasteur. There is no danger of losing oneself in the sloping streets of the new city or the medina. A great feeling of human warmth also reigns, as testified by the crowd of captivated admiring visitors and busy inhabitants who resolutely and quickly step along, the brilliant colors of the wares on exhibit inside and in the showcases of

the bazaar and the numberless shops often to be found in the most unexpected places, the perfume that floats around the tiny cafés where inhabitants and tourists alike come to sip their mint tea. Harmonius melodies, intermingled with the shouts of children, rise from the houses built on the hill in typically Arab style. It must also be kept in mind that the medina is a residential area where thousands of people live. To get an idea, one should begin a visit of the old city by leaving from the **Gran Socco**. This is the principal business square in the medina and is eternally animated. It is said that anything and everything can be bought and sold here which may be an exaggeration for Tangiers is no longer the international city it once was. Business however is flourishing and the wares on sale greatly varied: spices, gimcrackery, glass, textiles, chickens, fruit and vegetables, flowers, souvenirs. The shopkeepers seem to live in harmony with the pedlars and unauthorized vendors. The crowd is comprised of tourists, idlers, the inhabitants of the city and farmers from the surrounding regions. On market days in particular the farmers with their large red and white striped smocks, big hats with wool pompons and laced gaiters can be noted. Activity begins early in the morning and lasts till late. In the vicinity of the Grand Socco are the **Mendoubia Gardens**. The Palace was once the residence of the sultan's representative (Mendoub) in the city. Various 17th-century pieces of artillery can still be seen in the park. The minaret of the Sidi Bouabid mosque on the side opposite the Grand Socco is silhouetted against the sky. The elegance of this minaret lies in its pure, simple, sober forms.

Panorama of the port and bay of Tangiers with the walls
of the Kasbah and the Grand Socco (Place du 9 Avril),
the square which is the heart of the Medina.

Beyond the square, Rue es-Siaghin offers the possibility of admiring the jewellery in the showcases, authentic masterpieces which bear witness to the skill of the craftsmen and their sophisticated taste. Rings, bracelets, belts, brooches and other articles attract a numerous clientele. Continuing along this typical Maghreb street one finds oneself almost unexpectedly in a small square known as **Petit Socco**. These scenographic surroundings jealously guard various elements of the adventurous history of Tangiers. Hotels are concentrated here and the architecture of the cafés around the square recalls various European cities. Naturally the Petit Socco is no longer what it used to be before independence when businessmen, dealers and smugglers met here to make their «deals» in perfect peace and quiet. Today the square no longer has that feeling of enthusiasm and animation and has been invaded by vendors of craft products and souvenirs.

Rue de la Marine, in the immediate vicinity, will take us to the **Great Mosque**, built in the 17th century by Moulay Ismail on the site of the Portuguese cathedral that was then transformed into an Anglican church. This majestic building has an entrance decorated with tracery which stands out against the glazed majolica mosaics, protected by a shed roof in carved wood and painted with an inscription in Kuphic letters.

Opposite this monument, the architecture and decoration of a Merinid medrassa founded in the 14th century, attracts attention.

A few meters from the mosque and the medrassa is a terrace offering a panorama of the port. Rue de la Marine continues to the gate, Bab el-Bhar, and runs first into Rue Torres and then into Rue Raisoul which goes uphill towards the Kasbah. After passing a fountain decorated with majolica and carved stucowork, the Bab Al Assa leads to the Place de la Kasbah. At this point one can admire the Mosque of the Kasbah, the Law Courts (Dar ech-Chraa), the Royal Palace (Dar el-Makhzen) and the Treasury (Bit el-Mal), all of outstanding interest, in particular the **Royal Palace**, which was built by Moulay Ismail and enlarged by pasha Ahmed ben Ali around 1735, by Moulay Sliman in the early 1800s, and by the sultan Moulay el-Hassan in 1899.

The courtyard of the Palace is surrounded by arches decorated with glazed majolica resting on marble columns. The courtyard and the basin in the center are decorated with fine ceramics of Tetouan. The palace apartments, in excellent condition, house the **Museum of the Arts of Morocco**, with examples of craftwork from all the regions of the country: articles in wickerwork, vessels in brass, costumes, worked metals, jewellery, weapons, carpets, pottery, silk, painted wood, embroidery, musical instruments.

The palace known as **Dar Chorfas** (House of the Nobles) houses the **Museum of Antiquity**, with exhibitions of tools, weapons, coins and pictures that evoke the prehistoric and Roman eras of Morocco and in particular of the lovely city of Tangiers.

On the other hand, what names and what metaphors have not been used to celebrate Tangiers and its splendors! «The bride of the north», «the high city», «the bride of the straits», «the pearl of the north». These attributes accent its tourist riches. Is it not in the neighborhood that the waters of the Mediterranean and those of the Atlantic Ocean meet without mixing? As a result of this twofold influence the temperature is relatively stable. The

The refinement is a characteristic of the Moroccan hotels.

Panorama of Tangiers.

An evocative picture of the Caves of Hercules

beaches of Tangiers are ideal summer vacation spots for millions of visitors. For most tourists the city represents one of the major points of contact with Morocco. Tangiers offers at one and the same time the advantages of an exemplary seaside resort and those of a large modern city endowed with all the infrastructures required for rest, vacationing, sport, business and diversion. The top hotels run along the Mediterranean coastline with rooms that have a fine view of the beach and the **Avenue d'Espagne**. This boulevard can compete with the Promenade des Anglais which has made Niece famous. Flanked by palms and flowering gardens, the boulevard is unfortunately separated from the beach by a railroad. The inconveniences of this situation and the danger represented for the bathers have been under study and putting the solution into effect has become an urgent priority.

The Atlantic coast of Tangiers includes localities of rare beauty, with green wooded areas and infinite, often deserted, beaches. The **Caves of Hercules** are to be found 18 kilometers from Tangiers. Through this labyrinth of limestone rocks, flooded with water at every high tide, one can admire an unforgettable panorama over the Atlantic. It must be kept in mind that this coast is vulnerable and that the threat of wildcat urbanization hangs over it. Let us hope that this threat will never become reality. The projects now being carried out regarding Tangiers are reassuring. Thanks to its strategic position, the city is becoming the most European of the African cities. A permanent link via the strait of Gibraltar, on which numerous specialists have been working for years, will make the most of the tradition of Tangiers as a hinge city, confirming its international vocation.

Other economic, financial and social projects are destined to transform Tangiers in the immediate future into a place for free trade and cooperation, still further proof of the opening of Morocco towards other countries.

A view from on high of Tetouan.

TETOUAN

Tetouan today is a major tourist site. The enchantment of the city and its surroundings are the pride of contemporary Moroccan tourism.

In effect, Tetouan is a fascinating and splendid city. Its lovely white houses enliven the hill of Dersa, overlooking the fertile valley of the Oued Martil covered with eucalyptus trees, cypresses, almonds and orange trees.

Founded in 1307 by the Merinid sultan Abou Thabit, the city had become the lair of corsairs favored by the vicinity of the sea. Henry III of Castille put an end to this intolerable situation by completely destroying the city in 1399. At this point a difficult and obscure period set in for Tetouan. Reconstruction did not begin until the 16th century, by Muslims and Jews expelled from Andalusia. Two centuries later, the Alaouite sultan Moulay Ismail returned the city to the role it merited by transform-ing it into the principal trading center with the West. In 1857, Tetouan was besieged by the Spanish who occupied it between 1860 and 1862, making it the capital of their protectorate in the northern zone at the beginning of the 20th century.

The city still has traces of this period and the atmosphere is Andalusian. In its town planning, costumes style, jewellery, music and gastronomy, the art and traditions of Spain can be clearly felt.

But the city is also, and above all, an eminent site for Islam and Moroccan culture. Above the high wall which embrace the old city the minarets are silhouetted against the blue sky. Tetouan boasts a long cultural tradition and now has its own university named after one of the great Alaouite sultans, Sidi Mohammed ben Abdallah, a Museum of Moroccan Arts and Folklore, an Archaeological Museum where one can see the finds from the excavation

The Queen's Gate and the Mosque of Sidi Es Saidi in
Tetouan.

carried out in the old Roman cities of Lixus and
Tamuda, and a conservatory of Andalusian music.
The Tourist Festival held here every year attracts
artists, writers, Moroccan and foreign intellectuals
and helps maintain the traditional vocation of the
city as a place for cultural exchange.
A myriad of beaches and numerous seaside resorts
stretch out along the nearby Mediterranean coast for
about 50 kilometers: Martil, Cabonegro, Mdiq,
Kabila, Ksar ar Rimal, Marina, Restinga, etc. All
these places, full of people in summer, offer an opportunity to enjoy the delights and joys of summer.
The sun is tolerable, the transparent water is emer-
ald green, tourist facilities are of the best with hotels, bungalows, night clubs, single dwellings, shops,
sport installations. In a word, the region offers all
the ingredients needed for resting, enjoyment,
pleasure.

The picturesque town of Chechaouen.

The market where farmers wearing huge straw
hats come every day

CHECHAOUEN

Situated 59 kilometers from Tetouan, Chechaouen, called Xauen by the Spanish, is also known by the name of Chaouen or Chefchaouen.

Its foundation dates to the 15th century, by Sidi Ali ben Rashid. At 600 meters altitude it clings to the sides between two mountain massifs whose peaks reach 2000 meters. Today it is one of the principal cities in the Jbala region.

The name is of Berber origin and «ech Chaouen» means «the horns». The term is also used to indicate a rendezvous. The name was already known before the foundation of this city. A village and a river in the territory of the Haha tribe southeast of Marrakesh were called Chechaouen. Subsequently the name was used to designate what is now

Chechaouen, as well as the surrounding mountains and a river.

Historians affirm that the Romans had built the city of Appinum on the site of the city, while another Roman city, Blida, was not far off. The city walls of the latter are still extant.

In the 15th century, Sidi Ali ben Rashid, who succeeded his father as head of an independent principality, founded Chechaouen. The city was to serve as a base for the soldiers involved in the struggle against the Portuguese invaders, whom they attempted to thrust back to the north. After occupying Ceuta in 1415, the Portuguese attempted to extend their dominion to the bordering areas. The role assigned to Chechaouen is revealed by the urban lay-

The Kasbah, a typical corner and a partial view of the Great Mosque of Chechaouen.

out and the site, on the mountains, in a strategic position which sheltered the population from the war, at a considerable distance from subsequent attacks and the Portuguese zone of occupation. During this period, the Merinid dynasty was in crisis and was unable to guarantee the safety of the populations in the north. The inhabitants had to count on their own efforts in facing the enemy from outside and ensuring the continuity of the religious tradition in this part of the Muslim world. The Jihad was a duty and men of culture and religion mobilitated the population for this purpose. The Chorfa Alamiin, who live in the region, devoted themselves to this holy mission. Chechaouen was transformed into a true refuge and a center for assembling the combatants. A kasbah was built. Various buildings rose on the left bank of the Oued Chechaouen, before the right bank was chosen for reasons of safety in view of the floods and its proximity to the original village of the Chorfa Alamiin. Sidi Ali ben Rashid personally surveyed the construction works of the city. During his reign which lasted around 40 years, Chechaouen became quite

important in the field of culture and religion. The economy prospered, in particular after the arrival of Andalusian refugees. The city expanded until it had all of six districts: Souika, Kharrazin, Rif Andaluso, Rif Sebbanin, Ansar ans Souk.

The Wattasid sultan, Mohammed esh-Sheik, alarmed by the growing importance of the city and the independence of Sidi Ali ben Rashid, launched a merciless war against them. He destroyed a great part of Chechaouen and succeeded in defeating the prince. Thanks to the intervention of the Chorfa Alamiin and the Oulema, the sultan showed clemency, pardoning Sidi Ali ben Rashid and naming him «wali» (prefect) of the Ghomara. Subsequently the city passed under the control of the Saadians and the Alaouites. Moulay Ismail built the palace known as Dar el Makhzen. When the Spanish settled there in 1920, Chechaouen lost some of its mysterious charm, although it remained a particularly devout city.

In effect, Chechaouen has always been devout for a variety of reasons. Most of the inhabitants are Chorfa, descendents of the Prophet. Their behaviour both in public and in private is marked by dignity, respectability, uprightousness and sacrifice.

The city also contains a dozen sanctuaries which, with the passage of time, have become pilgrimage sites. Tangible traces of the cultural and religious influences that Chechaouen excercised in the region throughout the centuries still remain, such as mosques and medrassas, manuscripts, as well as tales and memories, which sometimes blend with legend and serve to perpetuate, both in the beliefs and in the conscience, that holiness which is one of the typical features of the city, resulting in a sense of peace, tranquility and serenity which are highly regarded.

Dominated by the mountains of the Rif, life in Chechaouen is accompanied by the murmur of a thousand brooks. In the city water flows in all directions, sometimes separating into slender streams which converge once more in splendid basins, irrigating the flowers and crops around the terraced houses in Andalusian style with their red tiled roofs and walls whitewashed a brilliant white, together with blue or intense ochre. The stepped roads, although narrow, are festive. The inhabitants are discreet, hospitable and courteous.

Inside the kasbah a flower garden is hidden behind the walls. **Place el-Makhzen** and **Place Uta el-Hammam** are particularly charming. The former, in the eastern part, is the heart and animated center of Chechaouen and is surrounded by shops arranged in terraces. It has a fine fountain and is dominated by a minaret built of bricks and crowned by a white lantern. Place Uta el-Haman, nearby, has a market twice a week, on Monday and Thursday. A double ramp leads from the square to the Great Mosque flanked by an octagonal minaret. The medina is amazing with its cobbled lanes that wind between the charming houses with their irregularly placed openings, joined every so often by masonry arches. The atmosphere is typically Spanish. It must also be kept in mind that the splendid waters of the Mediterranean are near.

Andalusian music is very popular in this charming city. A festival is organized each year offering classic compositions, often little known, to an ever growing audience. Crafts are also famous, in particular the spinning and weaving of wool. The textiles produced in this region are among the loveliest in Morocco. The same holds for the carpets. Painting on wood is highly developed in Chechaouen where

The white houses of picturesque Chechaouen.

one can admire the elegance and precision of the artisans, their mastery of color and design.

On leaving Chechaouen, the routes towards Tetouan, al Hoceima and Fez offer an opportunity for pleasant excursions in the Jebala region. On the way to Tetouan, the Oued Laou, the valley of the Oued Mitzall and the small dam of Nakhla on the Oued Hajar furnish splendid landscapes. For those who prefer history there is **Souk el Arba des Beni Hassen**. The Berbers who live there represent an important branch of the Ghomara tribe who converted to Islam in the 8th century and became famous for their strong opposition to the Almohads. Moreover one can pay homage to Moulay Abd eslam ben Mchich, one of the four «poles» of Islam, founder of the Chadilite doctrine and father of the Chorfa Alamiin. He is also considered the protector of the Jebala regions. His mausoleum is one of the most famous and popular pilgrim sites in Morocco.

Along the road to Tetouan one can also visit the site of Tamuda, founded in the 2nd century B.C. and where the Romans set up a fortified encampment four centuries later.

The route from Chechaouen to Al Hoceima runs along the Rif offering splendid panoramas and leads to a lovely cedar forest. The numerous passes include Bab Taza, Bab Berred and Bab Besen. The city of Ketama, at an altitude of 1700 meters, is particularly lovely. After the Bab Tisichen pass one can stop at Kalah Iris and Badis which overlook the Mediterranean and already herald the landscape of Al Hoceima.

The road that leads to Fez passes near the Valchiusana spring of Ras el-Ma, about seventy kilometers from the pleasant city of Ouazzane, whose zaouia represented an important instrument of political and religious influence for Morocco.

Two views of the «white city» of Asilah.

ASILAH

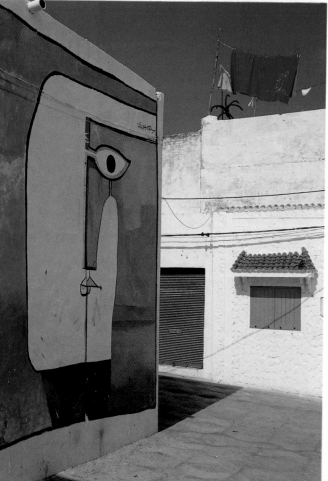

Around 40 kilometers from Tangiers on the route that leads to Rabat is Asilah, a small town with a rich historical past.

It was already known in Carthaginian times by the name of Arzila or Silis. In the period of the Mauretania Tingitana the coins struck there bore the name of the city in Punic characters. At present no trace is left of the Roman occupation on account of the numberless sieges to which the city was subjected from then on up to the beginning of the Idrissid dynasty. In the 14th century it became an extremely important port of call for the ships from Europe and recovered its past splendor. It was however occupied by the Portuguese in 1471, who transformed it into a military base for their troops. They were defeated in 1578 at the «Battle of the Three Kings». The Saadian sultan Ahmed el-Mansur forcefully freed the city from the subsequent Spanish occupation in 1589. A few years later the Spanish reconquered it but it was once more liberated by Moulay Ismail in 1691. From this date on the city once more became part of Morocco up to the Protectorate, despite the Austrian bombing of 1829 and the uprisings provoked by al Raissuni and his ill chosen allies near the end of the 1800s.

Today Asilah is a famous seaside resort. This pearl of the Atlantic has a constantly developing tourist infrastructure.

The old city (medina) seems to have come out of one of the tales of the thousand and one nights.

Asilah is also one of the localities artists and intellectuals prefer.

The annual festivals of the moussem give men of science and culture an occasion for encounters and exchange of ideas. The summer university and the African research center have given Asilah a new vocation, confirming at the same time that expression of its name which means «the authentic one».

AL HOCEIMA

Overlooking the placid waters of the Mediterranean, its back to the Rif montains, Al Hoceima offers a magnificent multi-colored spectacle. The blue of the sea, the gold of the fine coastal sand and the green of the trees on the Rif mountains lend a particular luminosity and fascination to the city and the bay. It is no wonder that the city is currently one of the most attractive seaside resorts in Morocco.

It is delightful to spend a few days in the hotels, bungalows, night clubs and camp sites where time passes happily. Particularly in summer when the days are filled with diversions on the beach and in sports and in the festive nights. There are a rich variety of gastronomic specialities. Fish is fresh and there is an intense activity on the fishing boats in the port of Al Hoceima but one can also go grouper fishing by oneself. Groupers are plentiful on this idyllic coast.

In the 18th century Al Hoceima and the islets which surround it like a necklace were contested by the French, the English and the Spaniards, all attracted by the strategic position of the site for military and trade purposes. Today the city and its isles offer the visitor their beauty and charm in an atmosphere of utter relaxation, a favorite tourist site, so marvelously endowed by nature.

Panorama of Al Hoceima.

A mosaic depicting Poseidon and the amphitheater of the archaeological zone of Lixus.

LIXUS

The ruins of Lixus, situated at the entrance to the city of Larache, preserve the splendor and the remembrance of an important period in the history of Morocco.

The foundation of Lixus goes back to the year 1100 B.C., when the Carthaginians set up a flourishing trading post there centered on the salting of fish and the production of garum (a sort of concentrated anchovy seasoning sauce).

Around 45 A.D. it became a Roman colony and continued to develop up to the 3rd century A.D., when Diocletian reorganized the Empire and it entered a phase of decline. The colonists on whom its prosperity depended left and the only reason why it continued to be occupied until the 5th century was its geographic position. The vestiges of this period can still be seen in situ and in the Archaeological Museum of Tetouan.

An outstandingly beautiful monument stands on the heights above Lixus. The hemicycle leads one to think that it was an **amphitheatre** with a circular pit

3.60 meters deep as arena. It was built against the hillside with the steps divided into sectors by staircases to facilitate the flow of spectators.

The adjacent bathing establishment, built at a later date, has a mosaic pavement depicting an enormous head of Poseidon, the deified ocean. This majestic mosaic provides the visitor to Lixus with still another source of wonder.

LARACHE

Larache is around forty kilometers from Asilah and is also bathed by the waters of the Atlantic. It was founded by the Merinid sultan Yusuf ben Ali in 1258 and since then its history has been characterized by an alternation of foreign occupations, in particular Spain, and liberation at the hands of Moroccan authorities. The port and its aperture to the sea have made the city a strategic point of primary importance. Larache is also situated at the entrance to a fertile valley where, according to legend, the Garden of the Hesperides was located. Nowadays this humid plain subject to floods favors the development of modern agriculture: vegetables, citrus fruits, sugar beets, rice, tea. The port has become even more important thanks to tunny fishing. From April to August, the tunny nets are installed offshore for this is when the banks of tunnyfish return north. As a result numerous industries for the preservation of the catch have been developed and constitute one of the principal activities, providing employment for many women.

The port is dominated by the Castle of the Storks, built by Philip III of Spain at the beginning of the 17th century. An imposing kasbah stands on the highest point of Larache. Between the two is the medina with its animated souk along a broad street lined by shops protected by fine arcades.

Panorama of Larache.

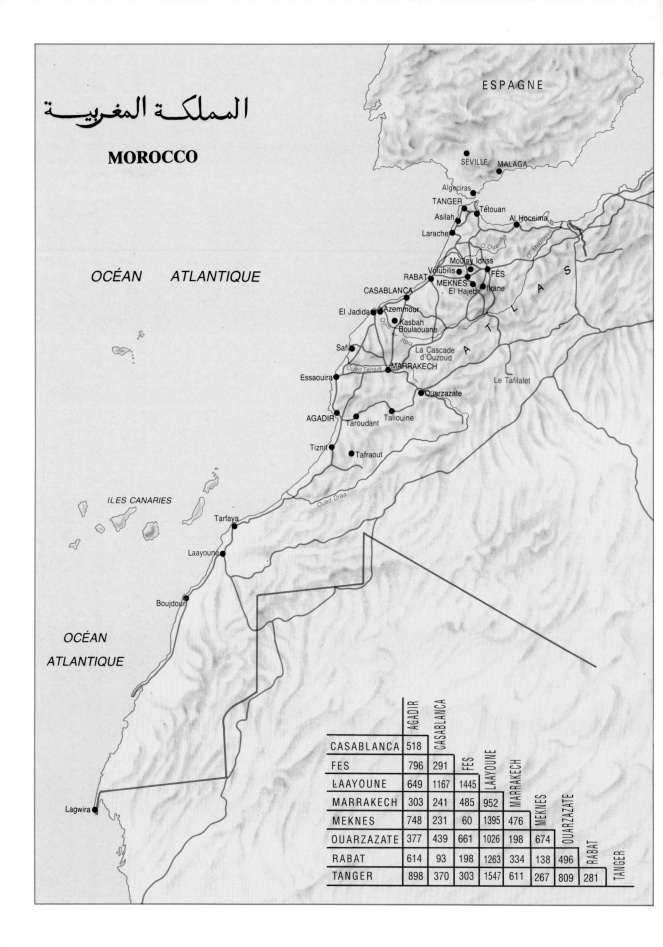

MOROCCO

المملكة المغربية

	AGADIR	CASABLANCA	FES	LAAYOUNE	MARRAKECH	MEKNES	OUARZAZATE	RABAT	TANGER
CASABLANCA	518								
FES	796	291							
LAAYOUNE	649	1167	1445						
MARRAKECH	303	241	485	952					
MEKNES	748	231	60	1395	476				
OUARZAZATE	377	439	661	1026	198	674			
RABAT	614	93	198	1263	334	138	496		
TANGER	898	370	303	1547	611	267	809	281	